dirty details

D0826568

marion deutsche cohen

dirty details

the days and nights of a well spouse

foreword by
marty wyngaarden krauss

temple university press
philadelphia

MIDDLEBURY COLLEGE LIBRARY

Temple University Press, Philadelphia 19122
Copyright © 1996 by Temple University. All rights reserved
Published 1996
Printed in the United States of America

∞The paper used in this publication meets the requirements
of the American National Standard for Information Sciences—
Permanence of Paper for Printed Library Materials,
ANSI Z39.48-1984

Text design by Arlene Putterman

Library of Congress Cataloging-in-Publication Data

Cohen, Marion Deutsche, 1943–
    Dirty details : the days and nights of a well spouse / Marion
Deutsche Cohen ; foreword by Marty Wyngaarden Krauss.
        p. cm.
    ISBN 1-56639-425-2 (cloth: alk. paper). — ISBN 1-56639-426-0
(paper: alk. paper)
    1. Cohen, Marion Deutsche, 1943–   2. Cohen, Jeffrey M.—
Health. 3. Multiple sclerosis—Patients—United States—Family
relationships. 4. Multiple sclerosis—Patients—United States—
Biography. I. Title.
RC377.C54 1996
362.1′96834′0092—dc20
    [B]   95-42473

contents

foreword

Dear reader, be prepared. This is a powerful and stirring book. It is unsparing in its honesty, its bluntness, its directness. Marion Cohen pulls us, willingly or not, into the daily life experiences of being the well spouse of a person with a debilitating and messy disability. She does so with little patience for the obfuscation of the harsh realities of transportation, communication, dressing, feeding, and, indeed, toileting that so frequently accompanies other tales of care giving. This book is almost a rebuttal to the comforting impression held by so many that there is a nobility in care giving that outweighs the mundane drudgery that it also entails. The anger that permeates parts of this book is at first overwhelming and, for some readers, may threaten to deflect the focus from the book's basic message. It is important to be prepared for this possibility.

Like me, you may find yourself working through many, many reactions to the story—reactions that may serve to help you dismiss the gripping dirty details that shock, fatigue, and confront you. I couldn't read this book in one sitting. I left it for days while I struggled with why I found it so hard to digest. Why was she so angry with everyone who tried, in their own manner, to be helpful? Why couldn't she say thank you to those who wanted to support her but couldn't make the commitment that she needed? Couldn't she see others' perspectives on her situation? How could she possibly have time for home schooling in the midst of her care-giving responsibilities? Was she pushing herself over the edge by being a writer, a lecturer, a teacher, a major-league nurturer of her children, AND a full time care giver? Where's the balance we so often invoke as the ticket to happiness? And, fitfully, Why can't she be more gracious about this situation? Ah, here's the real problem. We want our care givers to do their work with panache, with love, with nerves of steel, with dedication, and, please, without constant complaints. We don't really know how to deal with dire straits—as individuals, as communities, and as a society.

These are the ungenerous (and, in retrospect, embarrassing) reactions that the book can provoke in a reader who has yet to live the life Marion Cohen describes, who has yet to experience the "conspiracy of silence" that this book so brilliantly exposes, who has never needed to define "where I stand" regarding human endurance in impossible situations. This book ultimately puts the uninitiated reader on the defensive, as it forces a clearer examination of what we would do in Cohen's place. Now the anger starts to make sense. The "conspiracy of silence" feels pernicious, duplicitous, and horrible.

Cohen's description of her struggle to know where she stands clarifies her purpose. Her plea is for both self-knowledge (How much could and should she endure?) and professional honesty (What are the options?). This is the challenge she presents to the silent conspirators, and to society at large. Her plea reflects the need to calibrate her deep reservoir of energy and commitment to her husband with the options that might be presented to her in a nonconspiratorial world. One senses that even if she had known how to move on different options sooner, she would still have had to go through the process of facing and enduring dire straits before she could know where she stood.

This is the central dilemma. Care giving is an intensely personal issue that people do either because they want to (our emotional bonds fuel this reason) or because they have to (the conspiracy of silence helps here). People's stamina and tolerance vary immensely and reflect deep notions of personal responsibility, the prior history of the relationship, and cultural or societal expectations. The limits of care giving also reflect, however, the options that we design and support as part of the health-care system. When we exhaust people who are care givers by making them endure dire straits in order to prove their need for relief, we push people beyond their sensibilities and engender the kind of anger and bitterness that mark strong sections of this book. It could be so different. To help readers understand and internalize this message, Marion Cohen had to make us part of her family, her struggle, her despair. One emerges much clearer about the desperate need to be nonconspiratorial about the realities of care giving.

Thus, this book serves as a wake-up call about the limits of family-based care giving. For other well spouses, the authenticity of Cohen's frank discussion will air and validate the private and often hidden frustrations they have endured. The humor Cohen reveals about many aspects of care giving may also help people laugh at or lighten up on our social prohibitions against discussing unmentionable daily events. This book should send professionals and those who try to help well spouses straight to their mirrors to ask themselves whether they are contributing to the conspiracy of silence or helping to break it. For other readers who have not (yet) experienced the dire straits described so compellingly, this book provides a crash course in the dilemmas of disability, love, and human needs.

So, dear reader, you're in for a journey. The journey has its share of pathos, humor, and agony. Along the way, you are likely both to bond with and to disconnect from the story. Ultimately, however, Cohen forces our hand—where do we stand, as individuals and as a society, with respect to sharing the task of care giving? More than an interesting issue or simply something to ponder, this is as vital a reality for millions of families as anything most of us will know or experience. Marion Cohen's gift to us is that we'll never again be able to idly pass a person on a respirator, or with mental disabilities, or being pushed in a wheelchair without wondering about the person regulating the respirator, supporting those whose mental faculties are askew, or pushing the wheelchair. Our humanity has been enriched. Our conscience has been stirred. Our resolve to action? I hope it will be compassionate and swift.

Marty Wyngaarden Krauss
Brandeis University

preface

Some people have told me that this book is upsetting and hard to read. The "dirty details" are, for many, not only too dirty but too detailed. Why would one read such things? How could I write them?

When I was eleven, and my sister four years younger, we decided to imitate Anne Frank and keep diaries. Many evenings for years afterwards we sat up in our parallel beds, silently writing. I wrote about my adolescent loneliness, stresses at my suburban but tough junior high school, and the striving to grow up and connect. In some sense I wrote the dirty details. I wrote about math, the subject that had captured my imagination and my heart—geometry with its points and lines nudging each other, and algebra with its little x's and y's crawling around like frightened insects. And often I was aware that my sister was in the parallel bed writing *her* private thoughts.

By age fifteen I was also writing about Joe, my first secret crush, too shy even to talk to girls. Soon the pages filled up with John, Bernie, Connie, and then Jeff, an electrical engineering student who eventually made me girlfriend, fiancée, wife, mother—and well spouse.

When Jeff and I began to fall in love, I showed him my diary. I wanted him to know my thoughts—those I had not yet spoken, and those I was somehow afraid I would forget to tell him. Jeff *wanted* to know my thoughts. He'd take the diary home and read it, even the parts about him. Or we'd sit at my parents' kitchen table, he reading the diary, me doing math problems.

After a while, as writers in love sometimes do, I decided that now that I had Jeff to talk with—to be patient, understanding, and comforting—I could discontinue my diary. Instead I wrote letters to Jeff that resembled diary outpourings. When I finished college and we were able to marry, these letters stopped.

Occasions still arose when I realized that I needed to record my thoughts, but I wrote only on separate sheets, nothing as committed as a notebook or diary. Briefly in 1969, nine months before the birth of our first child, Marielle, I began a "pregnancy diary" and in 1973, another temporary diary about the birth of our second child, Arin.

In the midseventies, as part of my involvement in the women's movement, I began taking a women's writing workshop. We wrote about our experiences and beliefs; we read to, responded to, and affirmed each other. In particular, some of my ideas about the position of mothers and children in our society were interesting to the other mothers in the workshop. I realized that writing was a way to communicate not only with oneself, and not only with loved ones. I began to see that what I wrote could be helpful to many women—to many people.

I wrote poetry and articles, and I also reactivated my diary. Shortly afterward, two events in the winter of 1977 made diary writing a necessity for me. In October, Jeff was diagnosed as having multiple sclerosis. In December, Kerin, our third baby, died at the age of two days.

Kerin, not the MS, took over my diary pages, because she was more immediate, more in the present; the MS symptoms were still relatively mild. Eventually, this diary writing translated into "Kerin poems," which I was asked to read at the pregnancy-loss support group to which we belonged. The poems began to appear in bereaved-parent publications. I was invited to read them at conferences on death and dying, and eventually a small book of them was published.

I received letters that moved me. "Your books helped me more than both my therapist and my support group." "If not for you, I would not be sane." It seems to me that what I gave my readers—what they so urgently craved—was not only a passionate demonstration of the stages of grief, but the details: trying to get pregnant again, figuring out when I was ovulating. I supplied plenty of details, and some of them could be construed as dirty.

Jeff was interested in and proud of my writings about Kerin. He came to my readings and got to know some audience members; he was part of my audience. When the pregnancy-loss repercussions had subsided and when, around 1982, his MS began to progress to the point where we were feeling it, I began writing about that in my diary, and then in poems. There was not always time to read all the poems to Jeff at the moment of writing, but he always

knew of their content because this content was whatever I
said around the house, whatever I talked to him about.

However, he had been in denial for a long time about his
illness, and at first he was hesitant about my publishing the
MS poems or reading them at MS support-group meetings.
"I'm not ready for that yet," he told me. Reluctantly, I
waited for him to tell me when he was ready. It was not a
long wait. Around 1983 he began having to use a wheelchair; also at that time we began family therapy. And at the
support-group meetings, the issue of denial came up. Jeff
began acknowledging and sharing his MS, and soon he was
ready for me to share it. ∎

A couple of years ago going public took another form. My
Brooklyn publisher, Roberta, put me in touch with a photographer, Anna Moon, who specializes in photographing
at-home care givers. Roberta soon obtained a grant that
would pay for a joint exhibit of Anna's photographs and my
MS poems, along with a chapbook of poetry and photos. Jeff
and I talked first. I knew that I certainly didn't want to pass
up the opportunity, and I was pretty sure Jeff would feel the
same way. I asked him anyway; would he think of it as
intrusive?

"No," he answered, "I think it'll be fun."

That's how I often think of it, too. Fun. I suppose that
sounds a bit odd, but people who have had experiences like
this seem to understand. Of course MS is no fun; of course
losing a newborn is no fun. But after a while these experiences become part of our life mix; we *want* them to. For me,
life in general—including the bad parts—is fun.

I wasn't surprised at Jeff's answer, nor was I surprised when he added, "I don't want anything below the belt, though." Perhaps this statement expresses metaphorically what I also feel.

As I was writing the MS poems, I also wrote about MS in my journal, and I realized that the poems and the prose did not overlap very much, that there were things in the prose I couldn't say in poetry. And so this book, *Dirty Details*, was conceived and gestated.

Immediately after the editor at Temple University Press called to let me know that the book had been accepted for publication, Jeff was the first one I called; he's the one I was most excited about calling. It was early enough for me to still be in the bedroom, dressed and having had my sufficient dose of morning writing, but not yet breakfasted. Nine-year-old Devin had slept with me the past night and still lay stretched out, eyes closed, breath slow and even.

"You're the third to know," I said to Jeff over the phone. "First Temple Press, then me, and now you."

Devin opened one eye. "Uh-uh. I was awake all that time. Dad's the *fourth* to know."

Devin likes to hear me tell that story, and I like to tell it when he's around.

On the train ride back from a recent four-day visit to Jeff's parents in North Jersey, I read Devin this introduction; I was interested in what he'd think of it, and I hoped he'd say something that would give me an idea for an ending. When I came to the part about calling Jeff to tell him of the placement of this book, Dev sat up a little straighter. "And did you write how I—"

"Oh, yes," I interrupted. "Listen. 'You're the third to know,' I said to Jeff over the phone. 'First Temple Press, then . . .'"

Devin settled back in apparent satisfaction. I thought how important details are. Not necessarily dirty details, just details. And I thought how writing has become, for me, a family affair.

dirty details

the trike and the 49 bus

one

We had it down pat. As soon as I'd hear that "Mar!" I'd yell back "Okay!" so I wouldn't have to hear it again. I'd hear it again anyway. "Mar! Toilet!" I'd sink; I'd shrug; I'd tantrum, to myself or aloud.

I'd race up the stairs and down the hall to Jeff's wheelchair, which we called "the trike." I'd unlock both brakes at the same time, spin around to the back, zoom through the two doors, enter the bathroom backwards and swing clear of the sink, then spin around in front and lock both brakes at the same time. As fast as possible, I'd undo Jeff's belt, un-Velcro his pants, pull off the side of the chair nearest the toilet (sometimes it would stick), brace his legs and then my legs (making sure he'd gotten hold of his pants), so he could push down while I pulled up. Then I'd bend down, lift his right arm around my back, make sure he could lift his left arm today. (His left arm was his good arm, then; he *had* a good arm, then.) Then I'd pull up and try to stay up so he could make sure his pants went down. Using both my knees I'd ease him down and onto the toilet, and steady him between my knees. (That was a discovery, using my knees

1

as though they were limbs.) I'd put the side of the chair back on so he could lean on it, and I'd put a jar on him, too, in case he'd need it for urinating ("toilet" meant defecation).

Then I'd go back to writing, typing, Scrabble with the kids, playing the piano, correcting calculus papers, or supper. I could, or at least I did, eat under those circumstances; one of the reasons I'd eat instead of wait for him was so I wouldn't be away from the supper table, and the kids, any more than I had to. "Ten minutes, okay?" I'd ask him, hoping he'd answer, "Okay," hoping he wouldn't say "I need you to balance me" or "Could you just scratch my left ear?"

In ten minutes, maybe fifteen, I'd run back up, hoping he'd say it had been a false alarm but knowing that if it had been he'd soon be calling "Mar!" again—and then there'd be two interruptions to dinner, at least. If it was a "success," as he'd call it, I'd pull him forward, leaving four inches of space between him and the inside back of the seat. I'd leave that space—that "steamy triengle," I called it in the title poem from *Epsilon Country*—for the paper to fall into, hoping it would fall and not get wedged in there.

Sometimes I'd pause at this point to look through the slightly open bathroom doorway at sleeping Devin, our child of those years, still a baby; I'd sneak a look at those almost blond curls and those Bubbalah hands lying gracefully in the most ungraceful positions; I'd sneak a peak or two at the happiness that got us through those years. Anyway, then I'd wipe, starting far enough down so I'd get it all, which would mean fewer wipes, and I'd pause again, pause and think back thirty years, to imagine my mother saying not "Have you and Jeff been petting?" but "Have you and

Jeff been wiping?" If she didn't approve of him then—I'd almost laugh when I thought of this—what would she think of him now?

To get him up again and the pants back on, we had a new trick (we were always having new tricks). I'd pull Jeff forward and all the way to the left so I could pull up his pants on the right side. Then I'd shift him all the way to the right so I could pull up the left side. Then I'd get in back and sort of juggle him a little, which would eventually bring up the middle of his pants. I'd buckle, then Velcro, then lift up his left arm and put it around me, then the right arm. I'd brace all four of our legs and lift, lift, lift him back into the trike. It was higher than the toilet seat so I'd have to grab onto the grab bar with half a hand. I'd run him back to the bedroom, and remember to put him close enough to the phone, that lifeline. Otherwise I'd be hearing that "Mar!" as soon as I was settled back at dinner. I'd set the little table in front of him and there we'd be, right back where we'd started minus what I'd just flushed or wiped.

That was in the days when he could call "Mar!" loud enough for me to hear him from downstairs, when there didn't have to be someone upstairs with him at all times, when he could still answer the phone if not dial, and when he still lived at home. It was, even then, the speaker phone, the same one he uses now at Inglis House, the nursing home, although today someone has to be in his room in order for him to answer and still his voice comes through pretty weak. That was in the days when he could sit up in the trike all day, when he had the energy, if not the ability, to shift at least slightly so his behind wouldn't hurt.

4

It feels strange to think back to that time. It feels stranger to think back even further, to when our lives were "normal," "regular," and multiple sclerosis was a vague distant term; perhaps we'd heard of the MS Society, perhaps not. ∎

Jeff and I met on a bus in 1958; I was fifteen, he seventeen. Jeff was on his way home from what was then Newark College of Engineering; I was returning from my day at Arts High, a music and art high school in Newark, New Jersey, to which I commuted from small-town Roselle, because I played the piano and because I'd been miserable at Roselle High. Jeff picked me out, he likes to remember, because I "looked cute"; he put his books down on the seat next to him so no one else could sit there, then he removed the books for me. We wound up talking about our common interest in math, in particular about the book *Flatland*, George Abbott's nineteenth-century fantasy about worlds of both less and more than three dimensions. (The person who wrote the introduction to that book, and who is to be credited for bringing it back into circulation, would later be a physics colleague of Jeff's.)

It took Jeff and me a year and a half to start dating, but we kept meeting on that number 49 bus and talking about math. It was never acknowledged but always in the air that we meant something to each other, that eventually we would wind up together.

Our relationship was one of both minds and bodies. We talked about everything; there were no secrets (at least no conscious secrets). Since the day we finally said that we loved each other and would be joining our lives, I have never been lonely. When we went to the movies together, I couldn't concentrate on the movie, only on him. No one in the history of the world, I thought, had ever loved so intensely and so meaningfully.

I finished Arts High and received a full-tuition-plus-fees scholarship at New York University as a math major; Jeff finished NCE, landed a physics fellowship at Yale, and settled into the study of Einstein's theory of relativity, probably partly through my influence. We saw each other on weekends; eventually I got a fellowship at Wesleyan's graduate math department and we married in a small but typical Jewish ceremony that we both enjoyed (I'm not sure how many people enjoy their own weddings).

In the first couple of years of married life, we experienced some minor stresses, the kind young people worry over. We had landlady troubles, stopped the rent check, and wound up getting sued. Jeff got a speeding ticket—seventy-two miles per hour in a fifty-five zone; he contested it but lost his license for a month, and I had to get *my* license to get him to his classes.

And then two brief medical episodes occurred. First, Jeff experienced a week of blurred vision—"blindness," he called it. The doctor at Student Health could offer no treatment or explanation; the "blindness" simply disappeared. Second, Jeff had tingly fingertips for a few weeks. The doctor prescribed niacin—nicotinic acid—which did the trick (or maybe the tingles just went away by themselves). In retrospect, the doctor probably knew Jeff had MS but didn't tell us; doctors often hate diagnosing MS because there's little that can be done about it. A friend recently confided that a doctor she knows told her that temporary blindness is almost a sure-fire symptom of MS. Neither episode worried me at the time, although they did worry Jeff.

The next eleven or twelve years passed relatively normally. Jeff received his Ph.D. and took a postdoctoral fellowship at Yale. We went to lots of government-funded physics conferences that involved stays in posh hotels like the Fountainbleu in Miami, meals in French restaurants, and trips to Europe. Then Jeff received an Institute for Space Studies fellowship, which meant two great years in our favorite place, New York City. Meanwhile, I was having troubles with the Wesleyan math department. Since no faculty member specialized in distribution theory, my chosen thesis topic, I was advised to find an advisor outside the university and was offered no help in doing so. I spent three years searching, worrying, and feeling even more inadequate than the average graduate student. With Jeff's help, I did find an in absentia thesis advisor, world-famous mathematician Laurent Schwartz, who in fact was the inventor of my topic. In 1969 I got both my Ph.D. and my first child, Marielle, whom we brought to the thesis defense.

In 1973 our first son, Arin, was born. Jeff spent two years at the Institute for Advanced Study in Princeton; he published prodigiously, developed the theory of the dragging of inertial frames, quickly won a reputation in his field, and earned tenure at the University of Pennsylvania in Philadelphia. My math career proceeded less dramatically; I published seven papers in professional journals, most of them with Jeff, but several job disappointments caused me anxiety and anguish. I was also becoming increasingly and happily involved with being a mother—not so much the work of it as the wonder of it.

Despite un- or underemployment and despite repeated rejection by academic journals, I continued to do math research in both Schwartz distribution theory and an abstract concept that I invented and dubbed "pseudo order type maps." I was active in the women's movement; I had joined the Association for Women in Mathematics, and I wrote for their newsletter. I began teaching a math-anxiety workshop at what was then the Continuing Education for Women program at Temple University Center City, and I joined a women's writing workshop that encouraged and inspired my writing. I developed a feminist theory of motherhood, gained a small local reputation for this, and wrote for feminist publications. (Capsulized, my politics of motherhood theory runs: Mothers constitute an oppressed class, and/but this is not a reason for women not to want to be mothers—for *mothers* substitute *Blacks, lesbians,* or *women.* Nowadays I talk about being "mother-identified.") I also taught at the Free Women's School, wrote and published poetry, coordinated poetry readings at the Bicentennial Women's Center, and coedited an anthology of women's writings. I was, in other words, involved in small, mostly non-money-making endeavors.

Jeff was supportive, both emotionally and financially, during that period (and now, even in the nursing home, he still supports the kids and me financially via his physics research). He would have liked me to share the financial burden, and I felt guilt and ambivalence about not doing so. That was a strange era—a transitional time, as I think back upon it.

We shared our lives, with their various ordinary issues and stresses; we communicated and stuck together, and for eleven years there was no further "blindness" or tingly fingertips. One spring afternoon in 1975 we decided to see a movie playing about ten miles away. It was sunny and warm. We walked for three hours, stopping at one or two thrift shops. I wasn't the slightest bit tired, but Jeff, by the last stretch, was beginning to drag. "Can I lean on you?" he asked. A strange but isolated episode, and soon forgotten, at least for a while.

In 1977 we happily embarked on a third pregnancy. Elle was seven, Arin was four; I was teaching my math-anxiety workshop, plus a graduate course one evening a week in advanced engineering mathematics at Drexel, and feeling satisfied enough about the state of my career. Even with horrible morning sickness for five months, I stayed happy. But Jeff had begun having symptoms that didn't go away. The first was fatigue after supper, with no second wind at 10:00 P.M. The other was that, when we went out walking, he could manage only two or three blocks before he needed to lean on my shoulder or stop to rest.

"Adrenaline deficiency," said one doctor. "Some kind of flu," said another. Again, both doctors probably knew the truth.

Months passed. My morning sickness subsided and finally disappeared. I felt great and began combing the thrift stores for maternity and then baby clothes. I also sent my politics of motherhood book out to publishers; one indicated interest.

Jeff was having trouble with his handwriting; at the bank he took a full minute to sign a check, and I sometimes became impatient. We saw more doctors. Jeff bought *Current Medical Diagnosis and Treatment* and began looking up diseases and symptoms. One day he said to me, "I think I know what I have. I think I have MS."

A neurologist at the University of Pennsylvania hospital recommended a brain scan. I was seven months pregnant when we went together for that test; the test is painless, and we all joked around. But Jeff's self-diagnosis was confirmed.

I remember the moment. Jeff was not devastated. "So," he said, "the doctor says I'll probably live about another twenty years; that's a pretty long time." Twenty years *is* a long time. And two months seemed, at that moment, even longer—the two months until the baby would be born. In other words, I was too caught up in that pregnancy to be devastated about a diagnosis that was not affecting us in any big way right then. A couple of days ago I asked Jeff, "Did you feel that I ignored you when you were first diagnosed?" When he answered no, I was relieved. I continued to feel relieved, even after he added, "I did feel that I needed to be diagnosed before you would believe I was sick."

Once Jeff had gotten his diagnosis, he seemed to want to forget it, at least on some levels. The symptoms, he would say, were not the MS but a result of poor diet. To that end he tried one health diet after another, as well as one after another of the many holistic health methods he was reading about. Certainly he wanted to deny having the condition.

Mainly, he did not want anyone except his doctor and me to know. His parents, my parents, our children . . . he asked me to please not tell. For a long time, I figured that it was his disease and that his needs took precedence.

And what of the two months? The two months, that is, between the diagnosis and my due date. Well, they passed. There were problems with the birth, and our baby girl, Kerin, died at the age of two days. It was not because of any unconscious upset on my part over Jeff's diagnosis. I had my own diagnosis: I had a tendency toward postmaturity, which means the placenta starts to deteriorate before labor starts. There had been indications in my first two pregnancies that my obstetricians had failed to warn me about.

I was devastated. Living was hell. Jeff's MS took a back seat in my mind. I put my energy into mourning and into planning for another baby. Jeff told me that yes, of course, we would try for another baby, but what he cared about most was finding a cure for MS. Our different perspectives saddened us, perhaps scared us, but we talked about them; each talked about that thing into which we were putting energy. I felt that Jeff was there both with me and for me in that terrible time. I might not have been with him in his grieving (however denied), but he was with me in mine.

Eight and a half months later my subsequent pregnancy was confirmed, and I felt much better. Although I still grieved for Kerin, I stopped grieving for myself. I was scared, but the happiness was more intense than the fear. Exactly on the due date, with the help of my high-risk-pregnancy doctors, pitocen, and then an emergency C-section, Bret was born.

Jeff's symptoms were escalating only slightly. To me and the kids, they were mere inconveniences; we had to bring him books across the room, sometimes take dictation, and bow to his various diets and their paraphernalia (in particular, on our kitchen counter, a forty-pound carrot juicer called "the food factory"). When we were out walking for more than a block, he would lean on my shoulders. "I've been sick lately," he'd explain to the kids, or "I had too many milkshakes when I was little." And to passersby on the streets, "I hurt myself on the subway." It was ridiculous.

When Bret was three and a half, Jeff finally admitted to needing a motorized wheelchair. And although the whole family immediately called it "the trike," Jeff had to stop denying. Besides, we had joined an MS support group and had begun therapy (initially because one of our kids was having, understandably, a behavior problem). I had started writing about my own experience with Jeff's MS, and I wanted to read what I wrote at the support group. Jeff was forced to realize how ridiculous his denial was. We told the kids, his parents, my sister, and various friends. The honesty felt good to me; it was almost a high. And the minor inconveniences seemed even more minor. We felt less alone, and I think I must have believed that, now that everyone knew, they would help out if and when we needed them. I didn't realize it wasn't that simple.

Of course life continued to get less and less "normal," less and less "regular." The trike had to be charged. Someone had to help Jeff charge it. Sometimes, in the middle of all those South Street stores and restaurants that like many other Philadelphians, we so enjoyed, it would run out of charge. Or it would break. Or it wouldn't fit inside our favorite restaurant. Or the bus driver wouldn't let us on; he'd say only manual wheelchairs were allowed. And when we got back home, we had to pull the 120-pound trike up the front steps.

When did Jeff start using jars at night? When, that is, did it become too difficult for him to get up and into the bathroom in time? It's hard to place in sequence. A lot of things are. MS is chronic, and Jeff's type of MS is "slow progressive," so it sneaked up on us. Inconvenience sneaked its way into stress, stress into "toilet." It's hard to know just when.

But Jeff continued his teaching and his research. In fact, in 1984 he solved a problem posed by Einstein forty years before, and he was written up, for example, on the front page of the *Philadelphia Inquirer.* To do all this, of course, involved more and more variables—the "handy van" that the University of Pennsylvania provided for its disabled students and staff, curb cuts, ramps, computers, colleagues (or me) to write up calculations, and eventually home-health aides. When was it (four years ago?) that the university arranged for a student to go into Jeff's classes to help with things like collecting papers? When did the small but frequent task of recording grades in his notebook fall to me?

In 1983 Bret was four and a half, and, despite the MS, we decided to have another baby. This was not a form of denial; we understood quite well what we were getting into. We simply wanted a baby, and we believed (and still do) that the MS was not a reason not to have one. Besides we all needed something nice to happen. What followed was four miscarriages over the next two years. During this period Jeff's MS slowly progressed, and I was terrified that he would no longer be able to fertilize my egg. I wrote miscarriage poems; we bought a house; once Jeff lost control and defecated in his father's car. But in 1985 we had Devin—Dewdrop, I called him those first few months.

Jeff was in the delivery room with me, but, as long labor evolved into longer labor, he became too tired and too hungry to be of much help. He kept asking for food and oxygen for *him.* At one point he fainted and fell off the trike. But he was still able, then, to take the trike by himself and visit me in the hospital. And he could hold the baby and, later, babysit. When the baby became a toddler, Jeff took him for rides on the trike; the two became a familiar pair around the neighborhood. Jeff also did more physics than ever, and I did more writing. My book, *Counting to Zero: Poems about Repeated Miscarriage,* was accepted for publication. I became aware that math, writing, and babies came from the same place inside me.

The MS progressed, and the normalcy of our lives regressed. I remember the approximate dates of those regressions in terms of Devin's age. For example, he was seven months old when Jeff began needing attendant care, at first only for buttoning his shirt in the morning. Devin was two and a half when it became the rule rather than the exception that his dad could not make it to and from the trike—that is, when "toilet" began. The year Devin was seven, I decided that I could not continue to lead this kind of life, nor did I want to.

The kids did not want to, either. That year, 1993, we all

decided that Dad wouldn't live at home anymore. He would live at Inglis House.

It feels strange to think back. Bus seat for two, toilet for two, and now huge king-sized bed for one. No more gradual, perhaps, than life in general. And, paradoxically, no more sudden, either. ■

nights, lifting, and toilet:
the first conspiracy of silence
two

everal friends don't understand why, at Inglis House, they don't put Jeff on the toilet, why they just wait for him to go and then clean him. They think that's terrible. But I've done toilet, and I know why.

I also know about the way they do handle it at Inglis House. That's no picnic, either. Only too well do I remember those nights, sometimes two or three times a night, never just in the bedpan, or even on the towel underneath the bedpan, but always on the sheets—both the top sheet and the bottom sheet—and sometimes on the mattress under the sheets.

I'd worry, Kafka-style. It's impossible to wring out the mattress. And the bed under the mattress. And the earth under the bed. I'd get upset, angry. Even Atlas couldn't wring out the earth. And—what was almost too delicious to contemplate or tantrum about—not only because there would be no place for what I wrung out to fall, but because there's simply too much of it. ■

It wasn't all toilet and bedpan. Jeff would have trouble using the phone, or he'd need someone to write down a number, an address, or an entire physics calculation. He always felt anxious and rushed about those physics-related phone calls and those calculations. They were his life and his livelihood, more and more so as he became less able to teach, as he was finally excused from his teaching duties, and as he knew that the University of Pennsylvania was paying him for research alone.

Most often it was a jar he'd need, or a page turned in a physics book. Still, when I heard "Mar!" I thought "toilet." I expected toilet. "Please," I'd mouth, "not toilet." And if it was only the jar, I'd think, "Oh," or I'd say, in a sarcastically pleasant tone, "Something *possible*? At your service!"

Usually I said exactly what I was thinking. It came naturally to me and seemed honest and healthy. It was my way. It is not the way of all well spouses; some keep their anger to themselves or express it less vocally and less often. For me, speaking my mind preserved my sanity and our relationship, and mine with the kids. It also seemed a way to let the kids know that they had permission (mine if not society's) to feel—to be angry, sad, upset, resentful, whatever.

As in my childhood household, my husband and children often talked about "Marion's temper tantrums" or "Mommy's temper tantrums," but for me tantrums and assertiveness went hand in hand. I never threw things, never hit anybody, often didn't even scream; long was what I got, not loud. My tantrums were a matter of words, sometimes quite eloquent. After a while, with help from therapy, Harriet Lerner's book "The Dance of Anger," and the writing of a series of anger poems, I got some hold on those tantrums, or what other people said were tantrums. Now that what I call the "impossibleships" are over, I do not have tantrums, nor do I have to work at not having them. The situation was not to be abided, and I feel no regret or shame over my old long-winded honesty.

At the last well-spouse meeting someone said, "I went up to my room and closed the door and screamed and screamed and screamed." In the latest well-spouse newsletter a woman wrote anonymously, "One day I found myself standing on the bed, hauling my husband up onto it and being so upset that I was almost—but fortunately not quite—driven to BITE HIS ARM!" Another anonymous well spouse gives a beautifully clear description of this kind of repression scenario: "Would I ever hit him? Of course not. It would not be appropriate to break into his splendid isolation, his dreadful specialness, with anything as rude and irrelevant as violence. I have begun to act like a proper servant, always on call but rarely noticed. Suddenly it all seems so odd, my life, an old British play on public television."

There's no question that anger, however expressed or repressed, is a huge part of the well-spouse experience. As my therapist told me, one of the functions of anger is to stimulate change, and when change cannot happen, the anger builds on itself. Yet, for the most part, anger is not considered polite in our society, and many well spouses report guilt or shame about feeling it, or about having specific angry thoughts—again, whether expressed or repressed. I figure it this way: If I'm going to feel guilty no matter what, I might as well go ahead and express! ∎

So much had to be done *slowly.* Otherwise, Jeff feared, he might go into spasms. Taking off a jar, stretching his right arm, it all had to be slow. When I lifted his arms over my shoulder so he could hang on, I had to lift them slowly. Then I had to lift *him* slowly. I couldn't rely on centrifugal, inertial, or any other natural force. I had to continually apply my own force, instant by instant. In the middle of the night, when I'd straighten his legs and then separate them to make him comfortable, it had to be slowly. I'd be anxious to go back to sleep, or to finish feeding Dev, who of course was also anxious, but it would have to be slowly.

I'm just not the slowly type. I work quickly, efficiently. When a professor at NYU assigned a term paper, I'd have it done that week. I wrote my math Ph.D. thesis before I found an advisor. I had my first baby in three and a half hours. I write poetry books, find publishers, then write several more poetry books before the first are published. In choral group I sightread well; I see and sense quickly, not slowly. Perhaps one of the reasons I like to shop in thrift stores is that there's no waiting, no ordering. It's my way to engage in what I sometimes call "the first-minute rush."

But even when I did things slowly for Jeff, I was doomed. If his leg jerked from a spasm, he'd think it was because I hadn't done the physical therapy slowly enough. Today at Inglis House, if the feeding tube gets dislodged, he says the nurse's aide jerked it or didn't do it the way he told her. I take her side. I almost always take her side. ■

The winter I had a broken ankle, Jeff was downstairs one late morning, and I was in bed upstairs. The attendant the agency funded us for several hours a day (not twenty-four, nor even eight) had just left. Bret, ten at the time, had taken

Dev, four, to the park. "I guess Jeff'll be okay," I was thinking. "He won't need anything; he just had breakfast." Then I
heard "Mar!" And it was not one but two major things: (1)
toilet, and (2) broken stairglide.

That stairglide was vital to our daily existence. It consisted of a moveable chair attached to an especially sturdy
bannister along our stairway. Jeff got up and down the stairs
by being transferred from the wheelchair to the stairglide
seat and then pushing a button, which set the seat in motion. The stairglide worked electronically, and sometimes,
like just now, it broke down.

He'd called the cops—"sick-assist," they call it—but his
need was urgent, and their response wasn't. When a cop
finally arrived, it turned out that cops don't do toilet. They
"can't." Anyway, he'd arrived too late. I got downstairs
sitting and sliding (remember, broken stairglide, broken
ankle), and then I had to wipe while the cop held him up, all
the while telling us how he'd got another call and we had
five minutes. He kept glancing at his watch.

"We really could use a bit more compassion," I told him.
"We have a *lot* of troubles." The poor cop nodded. Maybe
the troubles on his beeper were worse. ■

About the broken stairglide. You might not know that
"adaptive equipment" companies take advantage of disabled people and charge and fix far more than they need to.
And you definitely don't yet know the extent to which Jeff
is a do-it-yourselfer. He'd do just about anything to avoid
being dependent on those companies. Not only is he a pro-
lific theoretical physicist, he's a practical physicist, too,

although that practicality sometimes suffers because of his theoretical bent. Jeff thought up something to fix the stairglide temporarily. After four days, the repairman came to look it over, maybe fix it permanently. "What's all this?" he exclaimed. "Who's been fooling around with this? This is a really big job; I can't fix this. Whoever fixed this violated every electrical code in the book."

Jeff said to me, after the guy had left, "A wire just came loose, that's all." I didn't know whom to believe. I knew about equipment-repair companies, but I also knew Jeff. His bachelor's is in electrical engineering, his Ph.D. is in Einstein's theory of relativity, and his research is in his own theory of relativity, but it still seemed he so often got things wrong. And that was before I began to suspect that the MS was affecting his judgment.

Jeff would fix the stairglide himself, permanently, he said. I worried about the electrical code. I worried a lot. I still think about it, sometimes. Jeff's at Inglis House, but the stairglide is still here. What if his MS does us in, after all? ∎

I lifted. I *could* lift. When I had the broken ankle, I also had my answer to the question What if I couldn't? Every morning and every evening I had to worry about how Jeff would get up and how he'd get down. Worrying about who would care for little Devin got lost in that sauce. Weekdays the regular attendant would get Jeff up—unless his own son was in the hospital with convulsions, as happened the day after I broke the ankle. Weekends we were on our own. Every evening we were on our own.

We had friends, but we had to call and ask each time. No one said, "I'll be over at ten every Tuesday." We had strong friends but not enough of them, so we found ourselves calling the same friend every third day or so. Our oldest son was then sixteen. He filled in a lot and was resentful a lot. (He's the one who was four and a half when his father was diagnosed.) There were a few days when we found no one, and Jeff simply did not get out of bed, which had one advantage: We wouldn't have to put him in bed that evening.

And now I'm thinking, "I'll never have problems like that again." And it feels great. ■

No, it wasn't all toilet. Sometimes I had to brush Jeff's teeth. There'd be something caught in there, something, he'd say, between the two very back ones. I'd go get the special mechanical disability toothbrush, run it through the cold water, set it in motion, then go digging.

Some of his teeth were gold or silver. Some of them were just plain yellow. I didn't like thinking about it all running together, water and teeth. The toothbrush would be getting warmer. "I should," I'd think guiltily, "go back to the bathroom and fill it with cold water again." When I brush my own teeth I dip the brush into cold running water every few seconds; I can't stand warm toothbrushes.

Also, when I brush my own teeth I don't have to look at them. I just feel them, just brush, don't think about what it all looks like in there. "People aren't meant to brush other people's teeth," I'd reflect. "With all due respect to disability politics," I'd say to myself guiltily, "ykk."

Well, I did it, I ran my term, it's over; now the Inglis

House nurses do it, and I still say ykk. I never said ykk about toilet, any more than I'd say ykk to changing my babies' diapers, any more than I'd say ykk to being in the delivery room with my wife if I was the husband. No, toilet wasn't ykk; toilet was just hard. The cleaning and lifting were what I minded about toilet, not the shit. Shit was like dirt, no worse, no more ykk.

Toothbrushing, on the other hand . . . holding somebody else's saliva on a warm toothbrush, or dipping the brush in the glass of lukewarm water I'd sometimes bring into the room, and seeing that water get grey and buggy, like the transparent suction tube now . . . At the end of every meal, the nurse comes in to suction him, meaning to vacuum the excess food and saliva out of his mouth. Otherwise it might go down the wrong pipe into his lungs, and he'd aspirate it, or get pneumonia. Sometimes I'm there when they do it. Bits of green and brown pass through the transparent tube like bugs, like the things that floated in the glass of water I'd hold as I brushed his teeth. . . .

I think it was okay to find *one* thing ykk. The disability movement wouldn't mind that. I guess I did pretty well. ∎

Some little miscellaneous things were neither lifting nor toilet nor "Mar!" nor ykk but were still not fair. Blueberries, for instance. For ordinary families it's okay to buy a pint of blueberries with only some of them really good. You put them in a fancy bowl and let everyone pick for themselves and be polite and not avoid the bad ones. But for us, for Jeff, it wasn't okay. When you're feeding somebody blueberries, you feel funny putting the little tiny ones into the spoon or those hard partially green ones. Especially if he's watching you do it. The cook is the server is, in a sense, the eater. It's all too close for comfort. You can't get away with buying the regular blueberries. You have to buy the expensive hand-picked kind. You have to handpick everything. ■

It wasn't all toilet, phone, "slowly," broken stairglide, lifting, toothbrushing, and blueberries. I was on night duty every night—unpaid night duty—and of course I was on day duty every day, if not as care giver, then as a mother, writer, teacher, and person. The baby was two when night duty began. He slept in our bed, and I gladly and hormonally woke up several times a night to nurse him. But there was nothing either glad or hormonal about jars, bedpan, turn over, tuck in, and, later, respirator adjusting. I worried about the psychological effects of seldom being allowed to finish my dreams.

At first Jeff woke me two or three times a night, and on a few summer dawns when he'd awaken short of breath and terrified (which is what led to his getting the night respirator). Soon he was waking me five and six times a night for an increasing number of jars and for additional tasks like itch scratching and physical therapy when he spasmed. By the time I'd decided it all had to end—well, I never actually counted the number of times, he was waking me every fifteen minutes, with some two-hour gaps some nights. By then he had more equipment to be tended to, more needs to be met, mostly the night-respirator but also a special air mattress that made turning him next to impossible, along with ever-changing bedpan routines.

24

One night, soon before he went to Inglis House, I got one hour's sleep, total. The respirator alarm—not the high-pressure one, the *low*-pressure one, the one you have to stand up and turn off kept sounding in error. Finally I figured, "No point in turning it off; it'll just start up again." So I let it scream for an hour, and I joined in. "I'm not being treated like a human being," I screamed, "so I'm *not* a human being." Because the alarm had gone off umpteen times, I screamed umpteen times, while Jeff matter-of-factly kept telling me, "Turn it off, Mar. Mar, turn it off," and eventually, "Mar, I need to be stretched" (one of our words for physical therapy).

As usual, Devin in our bed slept through it all, and as usual watching him might have been what kept me from going completely off the edge. But I knew that, very probably, the other kids had awakened and were trembling—Bret, just twelve, mature for his age but still capable of being hugged; Arin, eighteen, sad and shrugging and not entirely capable of being hugged; and Marielle, twenty-one, fully grown, and genuinely concerned. Likewise, throughout the four floors of our big house, the seven cats were keeping a low profile.

At some point I began another refrain: "I'm not human so I don't hear and I don't care. I'm losing all human traits." But I could hear and I did care and I was human, so eventually I turned the alarm off. I thought, however, "How come nobody's coming? Don't *they* hear? Don't *they* care? Aren't *they* human?" It could have been a *Twilight Zone* episode.

Jeff would say he was tired, too, but it didn't seem that

way. He was a night person and I wasn't, and it mattered. He always wanted to go to bed at eleven, twelve, often later; P.M. would have turned to A.M. Many were the evenings I was desperately tired and would try to convince him to let me put him to bed. But he'd have a physics paper he wanted to work on—"Just one short calculation," he'd beg—or a phone call to make about his solar-collector invention, the one he could never get funding to manufacture or even to put on our roof. By the time I was allowed to put him to bed and an hour later get into bed myself, I'd be desperate to the point of tears—and tantrums.

The truth was, putting Jeff to bed was bad for me regardless of the hour. I hated doing it, and even early in the evening I was too tired. Evenings for me are meant for winding down, not winding up. So I was willing, if not anxious, to procrastinate, and the later it got, the more willing I became. When Jeff would say, "Just another ten minutes," I'd answer, "Sure," thinking, "Thank goodness. Not right now."

Whether I was too willing a victim, perhaps codependent, was a question that kept coming up. In fact, my therapist assured me, I was a very *bad* codependent. Our situation offered me many opportunities to be victimized or codependent. This bedtime dance might have been the only one I came remotely close to taking. ∎

There's a conspiracy of silence about nights, lifting, and toilet. No one wants to hear about nights, lifting, and toilet. Not even many well spouses from the National Well

Spouse Foundation talk about them. At least not at first. Or it doesn't occur to them to talk about nights, lifting, and toilet. Like eating and breathing, they take them for granted, so much a part of their lives are nights, lifting, and toilet.

A recent passage from an otherwise wonderful article by a well spouse tends, I believe, to cloak our situations in euphemisms. "The types of services care givers provide," it runs, "range from general housework to help with bathing, providing transportation and emotional support, and actual nursing care, such as changing bandages and administering medication."

"Help with bathing?" I exclaim. "Changing bandages?" The author mentions nights, but not lifting or toilet, even in dressed-up phrases. While she makes some astute and pertinent statements about well-spousery and at-home care givers, if we want to advocate for at-home care givers, if we want to convince people and politicians, we have got to spill the dirty details.

Yes, if I had to say it all in three words, those words would be *nights, lifting,* and *toilet.* If someone were to ask me, "What's it like to be a well spouse?" I would answer, "Nights, lifting, and toilet." If I were permitted to elaborate, I'd continue, "By *nights* I don't mean wiping his brow or lying awake in fear listening to or for his breathing. By *lifting* I don't mean dragging him by the feet along the floor. And by *toilet* I don't mean changing catheters."

The lumps don't always fit down the toilet. It would usually take several flushes. And Jeff would keep going; I'd think he was done and then he'd go more. He'd be at it thirty, forty-five minutes. I'd have to wait, sometimes holding up his head.

And nights, the jars, too, took awhile. Either I'd have to wait with each jar, I'd have to wake up twice, once to put the jar on, once to take it off. Or I'd have to hold the jar on the entire time; otherwise it would spill. With all this, I felt, in the middle of the night, too tired to go to the bathroom myself, or to write at night as some writers do. ■

Even after well spouses have talked about nights, lifting, and toilet, they haven't necessarily shared all. Four years ago at my first well-spouse convention, I met Fern Zeigler, a family therapist who is now a special well-spouse friend of mine. Fern once said to me, "I still don't know about everyone's everyday lives," so we each went over a typical day—as typical as a well-spouse day can be. I told her how, for example, I began most of my weekdays lying awake, around 8:30, waiting for Jeff, who had finally fallen into a deep sleep, to wake up and ask for something. When he did I'd also undo the respirator, wipe the nosepiece, empty the jars, and miss out on Dev's morning nursing. Soon we'd both be listening for the doorbell. If 9:00 arrived and it hadn't yet rung, one of us would say, "Well, Benny's a little late." If by 9:15 the doorbell was still silent, we'd venture, "I guess he's a *lot* late." Usually about 9:30, we knew that it wasn't late, it was never. So I'd hit the black phone book—A for Attendants—and call Benny's mother, sister, various other numbers he'd said we might be able to reach him at, and finally the service that funded us for Benny and might be able to find a replacement—but usually, at such short notice, not.

Fern's mornings were similar, and we got so involved talking about them that we never discussed the afternoons or evenings, not in that conversation. Only later did we talk about how our days depended on whether the home-health aide had shown. "No" meant we'd have to stay home all day. "Yes" meant we could go about our business, sometimes forgetting, at least temporarily, what we were being relieved of. There was always the worry that something was amiss, that perhaps we should call home and check. Fern could not stay late at work, or linger with a colleague, and I couldn't be in Rittenhouse Square with Dev at my favorite time; the hour between 5:00 and 6:00, when kids arrived from daycare or after-school activities, and their parents came from their jobs, and everyone seemed relaxed, and everything settled down. Neither Fern nor I could enjoy the end of the day, even for a few minutes, because we had to be back home by the attendant's quitting time. And then, as we walked up our front steps, we would often be seized by some last-minute panic. Had there been a problem with the attendants? Had our husbands been rushed to the hospital? Were they in the middle of toilet, and would we have to take over once the attendants left? What was waiting for us behind those front doors?

It was also in later conversations that Fern and I described our evenings. Suppers, which involved feeding our spouses, mouthful by mouthful, alternating their mouthfuls with our own mouthfuls. The after-dinner hours, often like the after-dinner hours of regular families but always with the looming prospect of toilet and always with the fear of some emergency. Always, too, the awareness that we couldn't quite wind down, that we had to stay awake to put our husbands to bed. Then, of course, our nights. ∎

Mostly the conspiracy of silence was among the doctors, social-workers, and, later, physical and occupational therapists who came into our home with increasing frequency, but never frequent enough. These people already knew about nights, lifting, and toilet, and they didn't seem to want to hear more. Several times I asked the doctor, "Couldn't Jeff take something to help him sleep?" With a perfectly straight face the man answered, "With the respirator that would be contraindicated." I did point out to him that, for me, waking up ten, twenty times a night would be "contraindicated," but he shrugged, or said, "Uh-huh," or otherwise acted as though he didn't hear me. Or actually didn't hear me.

On one occasion, for three nights in a row the low-pressure respirator alarm went off for no reason every half hour, sometimes every five minutes. When the guy from the respirator company finally arrived—around 2:00 or 3:00 A.M.—he quite matter-of-factly told us that it had to be that way, because otherwise Jeff would get too many breaths per second, or not enough breaths per second, I don't remember the details. What I remember is that the man was completely serious when he said it was supposed to be that way; I was supposed to be awakened and forced to get up every half-hour or every five minutes.

I don't go along with the conspiracy of silence. I said to the guy, "I see I get no sympathy."

He shrugged.

"No sympathy," I added, "and no compassion."

He shrugged again.

"What is it with you guys?" I went on. "Is it that you're so used to seeing people whose lives are hellish that you're immune to it?"

He might have shrugged again.

"We're used to it, too," I continued. "How come we're not immune to it?"

My point is, this conspiracy hurts care givers. It hurts our feelings. It hurts because it means that not only do we not get helped, we don't even get acknowledged.

Sometimes it makes us crazy. Are nights, lifting, and toilet true, or are we only imagining them? Are we doing them because we're not managing things right? Not tapping into the correct resources? (But how could that be? The moment Jeff was diagnosed in 1977 shouldn't the doctor who diagnosed him have been the correct resource, the best connection?) Should we be insisting that our relatives and friends help us? (And should we somehow know how to do such insisting effectively?) Maybe nights, lifting, and toilet are true but not really that bad; could they only seem bad because we're not doing them right?

Arin, then a teenager, asked, "When's the government gonna decide we've had enough and do something about it?" ■

One night around 3:30, after five or six respirator adjustments and two or three jars, I knew I wasn't going back to sleep. I lay there, wanting to let the tears come. To not wipe or blot them but let them irritate my face, let them leave their marks, their wounds.

Maybe open wounds. Like open bedsores. Once Jeff's open bedsore was the only way to get Blue Cross to pay for help for my broken ankle. "Maybe," I thought, "if I lie here and cry long enough, the scars will be red and open and maybe Blue Cross or the Office of Vocational Rehabilitation or some relative or friend or patron or social worker or somebody—*somebody*—will do something about them."

Another night, again around 3:30, after many, many jars and respirator adjustments and no sleep—*no* sleep—I called Jeff's doctor and left the message, "I cannot do this anymore. Cannot. I know I sound crazy, but I am not crazy. I'm sure that anyone in this position would be making this phone call. Something must be done. My own health cannot take this anymore. Something must be done."

What was done about that phone call—that is, what the doctor did about it—was not get back to me. A couple of days later I asked him if he got my message. "No," he answered. "I didn't." Was he lying, or had his answering machine joined the conspiracy of silence? ∎

dire straits
three

The period from Jeff's diagnosis in 1977 to mid-1988, when Jeff could no longer transfer from and to the wheelchair, might be described as one of stress. But during the nearly six years from then until he went into the nursing home, we were in full-blown dire straits.

Well spouses don't suffer ordinary stress; we do not need stress-management workshops. Calling dire straits stress undermines well spouses and makes us feel alienated and confused about where we stand. Jeff and I would watch movies about young love, or old love. When these movies were interrupted by toilet, I'd remark, "No love could survive this." He'd nod and look worried.

Among famous couples, in movies and in life, she nurses him, or he her, for months or for years, to either a happy or sad ending. But an ending.

In movies the verb *nurse* doesn't mean weight lifting many times a day. It doesn't mean being imprisoned. And it doesn't mean forever and ever, with everyone expecting you to. In particular, with nurses and physical therapists and other paid professionals coming into your home and showing you how and saying uh-huh and looking askance when you allude to what you've been doing—be it nights, lifting, and toilet or teaching calculus or writing poetry.

In one movie a nine-year-old boy cares for his paralyzed grandfather. We see the kid spooning warm soup into the old man's mouth, but we don't see toilet or lifting, because a nine year old can't lift a grandfather onto the toilet, or even onto the bedpan. Most people can't singlehandedly lift a grandfather onto a toilet or bedpan.

Roberta, my Brooklyn publisher and friend, sent me the book *Hanging On*, about the last year in the life of a stroke patient. "Maybe this will help," Roberta wrote. "Thanks," I wrote back, "but 'hanging on' for seven years is a bit different from 'hanging on' for just one year. It's different when it's a living man you're taking care of, rather than a dying one."

A story going around the well-spouse grapevine tells of a "well husband" who "hung on" for many years or decades. His wife eventually died and he eventually remarried. However, he warned his new wife that if she became chronically ill he would not stay with her; "I couldn't do it again," he said. Years later she did become chronically ill, and he did leave her. The way I see it, stress is something we can do again. In fact, stress is what people usually do again and again, what we often wisely and even happily accept as something that naturally goes with the territory whenever life gets interesting—new job, new marriage, new baby, and so on. Dire straits, however, are not something a wise person chooses to repeat. ■

Around 1987, our friends Sarah and Eddie bought a house. At the last minute the deal fell through; they had already given up their apartment, so they and their two year old moved in with a friend. Not only did the friend show no interest whatever in the baby, he also left all sorts of dangerous-for-babies junk around the place. Sarah cooked for all of them; suppertimes were sorry scenes. Eddie, Sarah, and the baby slept on a mattress surrounded by sharp metal paraphernalia. Then they all got the flu; it lasted for months. Now that it's stress I'm going through and not dire straits, their situation sounds horrendous. At the time it did not; I would have traded my nights for theirs, sleeping surrounded by sharp metal. They slept, were allowed to sleep.

The point is, their ordeal ended. They found another house, and they moved in. "Things are looking up," Sarah told me. How I longed for things to look up for Jeff and me, for it to be possible for things to look up—in months, years, even a decade. This minute, writing these words and knowing I won't be interrupted by "Mar!"—knowing I might be up late but once I do go to bed, I'll be allowed to sleep jarless and respiratorless until at least 9:00—I'm thinking, with supreme gratitude, "Things are looking up." ∎

People didn't understand. They weren't informed. When I tried to inform them, sometimes I succeeded. Sometimes I failed. One afternoon Jeff and I were taking Dev, then two and a half, to the park to ride a little yellow bike I'd gotten him at a yard sale. (That, of course, was in the "trike days," when Jeff could steer the trike himself unless he got overheated. We could still go out together as a family, although I was beginning to avoid it.) Dev was riding his little bike, Jeff was scooting alongside on his trike, and I was overseeing both riders. We had gone a block when Jeff informed us, "I don't feel very well."

"Uh-oh," I thought.

Another block and he said, "I think I'd better go home."

I knew that meant we all had better go home. Moreover, it meant me steer the trike for him, maybe holding him up as I steered—all the while keeping a sharp eye on Dev as he rode his bike and pushing the stroller I had brought for when he got tired. I began screaming to the skies. "Nobody," I screamed, "nobody could carry a man and a two year old at the same time. Nobody could. Not only me. Not only me. Nobody could. Nobody." Yes, again and again. Yes, out there. Especially out there. Because a part of me still believed that somebody out there would save us from all this. And because I was never a closet well spouse.

What actually happened was, a young woman came over to us—and she came on with what still strikes me as professional pep talk. "Hey, hey, *he-ey*," she called. "Take it easy. Life isn't all that bad. Look, you have the baby." She paused. "Now's the time to get some of your buddies to help you." Then, "Do you have the number of any support group?"

I kept shooting out answers. "We've been to every support group in the area, and some out of the area." "We started some of them." "You need more than buddies for this." "I am taking it easy, just not every minute of every day." "I know life isn't all that bad. Look, we had the baby!" "In fact," I concluded, "I'm a writer, a published poet, and two of my poetry books are about *this*."

People didn't and don't understand. They often seem to

assume that what we need is a shoulder to cry on. Once a social worker actually tried to *put* my head on her shoulder; I wriggled away and told her, "Look, I've cried before. I've talked about it before. I've acknowledged my feelings plenty." And, again, "In fact, I write books about them, and they're published."

Professionals often seem to assume lots of things about us—not only that we haven't expressed our feelings sufficiently, but that we're mousy or, just the opposite, bossy, or that we're not liberated, or that we're not professionals ourselves. Or that we do too much ("Take a day off," they say. "Do something nice for yourself."), or that it's possible to take a day off. Or that what we need is to get organized; if we'd just make a list, things would get organized. Mostly, professionals seem to assume that we're under stress rather than in dire straits. And being in such dire straits, we often find it hard to appreciate that they mean well. I appreciate that more now.

The woman on Spruce Street kept her distance as she talked to us. She didn't move toward the stroller and offer to wheel it while I wheeled Jeff. Or to wheel Jeff while I wheeled the stroller. Of course, the help I had been screaming for was not immediate help but long-range help, lasting help. Whenever people offered immediate help, I'd feel bitter. "What about the next time" I'd feel like asking, "and the times after that?" ∎

We did get some long-range help. We researched and networked and got assertive bordering on aggressive, and we got as much help as it was possible to get. Thinking about it now, its volume seems impressive. I imagine that readers will wonder why I'm writing this.

After all, the service funded us at no charge for, at the end, six hours a day on weekdays. (That's part of the conspiracy of silence; agencies seem to pretend that weekends and holidays don't exist.) And especially toward the end, several friend volunteers, along with some of Jeff's colleagues, helped, if not with jar, then with feeding, as well as with writing down physics calculations. At one point Beverly did every Tuesday night, and Colleen did two nights a week. (Beverly burned out after three months; Colleen lasted only slightly longer.) And after I called a family meeting (*I* had to call it, and I had to conduct it; I had to advocate for myself), we got financial help from family, enough to hire someone one or two nights a week. Not an RN, or an LPN, just a regular person willing to work for twenty dollars a night and to believe Jeff when he'd say, "I wake up maybe two or three times, sometimes not at all," and who kept on believing it, even once he'd started the job. Someone, in other words, who kept the conspiracy of silence. Jeff's parents helped us financially. So did my sister Rosalyn and my Aunt Faygie. Jeff's brother gave us one evening a week. Later, when Jeff's speech started to falter and when toilet got more difficult or more impossible, his brother began to call "Mar!"—or sometimes "Bret!" to our then twelve year old.

The help of friends and family could never be enough. I still did most of the nights, and I was never sure when someone else on duty would call "Mar!" or "Bret!" Most friends could not do lifting or toilet. Our house still smelled of bedpan sheets, and our washer still did many loads a day. In a poem I wrote, "One person, one family / cannot do this alone." In prose I would change that to "One support system cannot do this alone."

One friend, Aurelio, did not call "Mar!" Not ever, not even once. Five and a half years ago my friend Joan introduced us to this angel. Aurelio started out as Jeff's Saturday attendant and soon became a family friend. "The family lifesaver" is how I'd introduce him. Besides Jeffwork, Aurelio did housework, kidwork, cooking, dishes, and laundry. At a recent well-spouse meeting Fern brought in a quote that describes him: "There are times when what is needed is not someone who asks 'What can I do to help?' but someone who gets in there and does it." Aurelio is one of those capable, versatile people who are rare in any walk of life, and his personality merged essentially and perfectly with our family's. Off and on he has actually lived with us, exchanging his skills and his presence for board, keep, and a small stipend. Now that Jeff's at Inglis House Aurelio is still with us, and it's wonderful to have him do more things for the kids and me, rather than emergency lifting and toilet. He prevented me from going insane; he helped me survive. Without him I could not have done it—I would not have done it for so long. But even Aurelio eventually felt burned out. And even he was not enough. Four—maybe three— Aurelios might have been. ■

The very worst impossibleship was finding attendants. "Yes, that's the worst," agrees Fern, my well spouse friend. I remember how naive I was when, eight years ago, our first attendant walked in the door—tall, strong Ron. I thought he'd be with us for years; I thought he'd be our life. In fact, he was out of the picture only months later; one day some other man walked in. I don't even remember that the agency called to let us know.

We've since had perhaps thirty or forty attendants; I stopped counting long ago. So did Fern. As anyone in the health-care field knows, attendants are a downtrodden breed, probably because they get low pay, no benefits, no paid vacations, and so forth. They can also be pretty casual. One day they suddenly don't show. Or they gradually don't show; one day they're late, the next day they're later. Or one day they call in sick; the next day they don't come and they don't call in sick. They come from all walks of life, and many are needy, disturbed individuals. What they need is to feel helpful, but when it comes to the nitty-gritty of the job, and when it goes on and on for weeks, that need gets distorted. Or they get hurt in accidents, often drug-related ones, and sometimes get or already are disabled themselves. Or they realize that the service reports their earnings; their pay isn't under the table. They can't be on welfare and work for the service, even part-time. Each of our thirty or forty attendants, except for Aurelio and Benny, had a different reason or nonreason for not showing or for quitting soon after starting.

Some of the more remarkable attendants were instantly enamored of our family—the kids, the cats—and entranced by our situation, our struggle, Jeff's physics, my writing. They were too enamored, too entranced; they'd get friendly far too fast. "What you need is a man," Annabel told me, not knowing, and not asking, whether I felt I had one. Stan called me up especially to tell me, "This job is so therapeutic for me" in the midst of a quiet jarless moment when we were all on the big bed watching a video. And he wanted to elaborate. After five minutes I cut him short. "We'll see you Saturday." On Saturday he didn't show. The scariest was William. He'd talk to himself while we were around, and he'd call me by the pet names Jeff has for me, in what seemed to me a strange, sneering tone. I asked the service not to send him again, but once, years later, they forgot, and in William walked.

In our search for reliable attendants, we went through newspapers and the list provided by an agency called Resources for Living Independently, and we asked friends. Aurelio and Benny were the only two attendants who lasted. The stream of unreliable characters, and the stress of the search, sometimes seemed even worse than nights, lifting, and toilet. Sometimes I'd think, "Maybe we just shouldn't have attendants; maybe it would be easier if we just took it for granted that Mar will do it all the time." But I knew only too well that after two days of no attendant I'd go beserk.

Training new attendants—how well spouses hate it. The first day was infinitely worse than doing the job myself. I'd try to make it look easy. "You just put your knees like this and grab him around the waist . . . " As Jeff became more and more a deadweight, most of them couldn't do it. They'd try. I'd have to show or help them each day, before they'd finally realize and just fail to show. Or not realize, and I'd have to fire them. "The person has to be able to lift," we'd remind the agency, but the conspiracy of silence was too strong for us. And people who can lift are not easy to come by.

In the midst of training each prospective attendant, I'd sometimes bend down and whisper to Jeff, "Suppose she can't do it? Suppose they all can't do it. Suppose I'm the only one in the whole world who can do it?"

He'd answer, "I know what you mean."

To reassure ourselves we'd imagine the worst scenario: We never find an attendant, and I wind up with a life sentence, mayn't leave the house at all, not ever. Well, I'd tell myself, we could always have things come to us. We could form even more support groups; we could have meetings at our house. And music parties, writers' parties; we could become an artists' hangout, fill our home with poetry, Mozart, Sierra Club.

Except, I'd realize—and the weight of this was heavy—the thrift stores wouldn't come to us. My simplest relaxation, my least complicated passion. Nor, Jeff reminded me, do thrift stores put out mail-order catalogs. So even the service couldn't help us enough, hadn't mastered the art of locating attendants any more than we had. And sometimes it had other problems. One Christmas Eve we were all sitting around the table when the service called. Their last grant application had been rejected and everybody was being cut to two hours a day. The social worker Peggy's voice was sad and tired; she was spending her holiday making these bad-news phone calls. For me, the news meant our four year old being imprisoned, too. No more hanging out in Rittenhouse Square, or any other mother-toddler excursions. "Oh, no!" I screamed. "No! No! No!" That was not stress.

Another time Benny, the attendant we finally found (he'd been with us almost a year and he could lift), got mugged. At first we thought he'd be off the job for less than a month, so he and Jeff found a backup—a character, true, but she'd do in a pinch—and Benny continued to sign the agency forms, instead of the backup. This was against the rules, and the service had explained very clearly why, but Jeff and Benny chose to handle the situation that way because they were scared of rocking the boat. Benny was scared of losing his job. Jeff was scared the new temporary attendant wouldn't sign the forms. They were scared, and they hadn't gotten a handle on it.

They couldn't predict that Benny would wind up needing a halo, a metal concoction resembling the frame of a giant helmet, designed to prevent him from turning his head and snapping his spine. He would be out for six months and apply for public assistance. We were all quite upset one afternoon when Benny's social worker called our agency to verify that he hadn't been working. Of course, according to the service's records, Benny had been working because he'd been signing the forms.

In the course of straightening things out, the service again warned Jeff and Benny to inform them of whatever was going on. I was scared we'd lose the service and scared Benny would lose his assistance, because of us.

The new temporary attendant did not want to fill in the forms. We weren't sure why. She only shrugged when we asked her, and her body language told us not to ask again.

And the service never did find us another reliable and permanent attendant. Until Benny's halo came off, we settled for letting another character into our home two or three days a week. The rest of the time I did the care giving. And I was a basket case.

I understood that the service needed to be informed every time we needed a new attendant because of eventualities like Benny's public assistance. Also, they have to keep their records straight—and impressive—in order to get grants. But that policy controlled and restricted our lives. Every time any attendant was out for even a day, the backup, if we found one, had to be somebody who would or could sign those forms. And if Jeff had to go out of town (he could go out of town in those days; he was riding once a week to Princeton), he needed an attendant who could work the entire day instead of the usual four or six hours, and so it sometimes had to be a different attendant from the usual one. It got quite complicated.

"Maybe they should just give disabled people money," Jeff and I would say. "Then we could simply hire any attendant we wanted; it wouldn't be the agency's problem, whether or not the attendant signed the forms." In fact, we continued, we could use the money to do something else besides hiring attendants, something else to relieve the dire straits—hire a housekeeper, say, or a secretary for Jeff, since he couldn't write. Or we could use the money to hire me or one of the kids as attendants. Or we could just buy our family something nice to make up for the dire straits, like that Oriental rug we'd seen in the window at Seventeenth and Walnut. It may be hard or impossible to find attendants, but it's not hard to find other nice things. And it would have been helpful to know that if—when—an attendant couldn't be found, we would get some money; we would, that is, get something. ■

As it was, neither agency, friends, relatives, nor enemies could make a dent in the dire straits. And people kept calling it "stress." In Fern's words, they "just didn't get it," and I kept needing to set them straight. I needed to define *dire straits*, to keep defining *dire straits*. I needed to articulate better and better definitions. And I needed everyone to know those definitions.

All of this translated quite often into "Marion's temper tantrums." One evening we were expecting company for dinner. I had spent the afternoon concocting homemade veggie soup and Wings of Life salad, which involved marinated tofu, fresh-roasted nuts, lemon-sesame dressing, and Jeff calling "Mar!" just as the sesame seeds were dry sautéing. I felt marinated myself, and I was about to step into the shower when Jeff informed me in that matter of fact denying way that Dev had just jammed in the new VCR tape. The implication was that the three-day-old VCR was now broken. Now remember, Jeff is a do-it-yourselfer, only he can't do it himself anymore. Moreover, his toolbox is a do-it-yourselfer's toolbox, namely tools piled in, little rhyme or reason, no space in between, jammed up far worse than any broken VCR. It's that toolbox that needs fixing.

I overreacted—or it would seem like overreacting to anybody who'd just walked in and didn't know or understand the whole scenario. "No!" I screamed. "No! No! No! No! No!" I paused. Then "No!" I paused again, then "No!" again. I wanted to scream louder than ever before. I wanted to scream louder than the *next* time. I wanted to show every-one that this time it really was the last straw.

I had to keep screaming. I could not stop. I did not choose to stop. And then, in that same matter-of-fact tone—and I realize that one of the reasons I needed to scream was to make up for that tone of his—Jeff informed me, "The bell just rang."

It wasn't the company. It was the cops. Three of them. "Someone heard a woman screaming," they said.

I shrugged and told them, "A woman *was* screaming."

"Were . . . were you screaming?"

I shrugged again. "If you lived this life, with a husband sick like this for so long, you'd scream, too."

"Are you all right?" one of them asked.

I simply could not bring myself to say I was all right. I was not all right. I was locked in the house. I was in dire straits. I needed to be rescued. I kept shrugging until they left.

After I had calmed down, Jeff laughed. "They thought someone was beating you up."

He had told me how to fix the VCR without going into that toolbox. You just pull out the plug and then put it back and the tape pops out, just enough. I had tried that and it had worked.

But I answered seriously. "Someone was beating me up. Someone, or something, has been beating me up for a long, long time." ■

At one of the well-spouse meetings it seemed that Bill, one of the two men in the group, was trying to *solve* the problem. "Have you tried this?" "Did you ever try that?" He was, again, defining the problem as stress, rather than dire straits. Well spouses do it sometimes, too.

"You know," he said, "all this is really our fault, all of us. We could be helping each other."

Many of us became instantly livid and hysterical. "Are you kidding?" Debbie gasped. "You mean I have to baby-duty her husband, too? No thanks!"

"I have enough on my hands with Harry," laughed Flora. "I don't need Jeff, too."

On and on we went. "You can't do two of them." "It's not like baby-sitting." "Gads, I wouldn't ever go on vacation if I knew that meant I had to take somebody else's unwell spouse for a weekend." "One of my worst nightmares is having a whole roomful of them." "Besides"—this from me—"I'm modest. I wouldn't do it for anybody else."

At one point I told Bill, "You're blaming the victim," and across the room Elaine nodded. Later in the evening, after we had all been talking about our efforts to find help among friends, relatives, and social-work agencies, I turned to Bill and said, "See, we have tried—and this is as good as it gets." Bill nodded. ■

Jeff in his office at Princeton University
(Photo by Jerome Lewis)

47

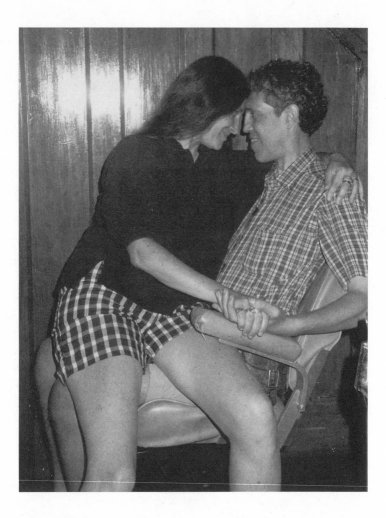

Jeff and I: the sitting-down hug
(Photo by Marielle Joy Cohen)

The same sitting-down hug
(Photo by Marielle Joy Cohen)

Jeff with Devin, aged three weeks
(Photo by Marion Cohen)

Bret, aged seven, trying out a new trike
(Photo by Marion Cohen)

51

A ride on the stairglide: Jeff with baby Devin
(Photo by Marion Cohen)

52

Jeff with baby Devin
(Photo by Marion Cohen)

53

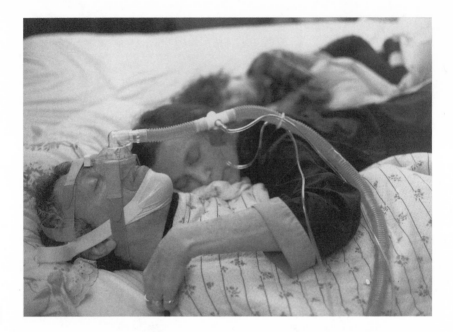

The lying-down hug
(Photo by Anna Kaufman Moon)

54

*The kids: Arin (twelve), Devin (baby), Marielle (sixteen), and
Bret (seven)
(Photo by Marion Cohen)*

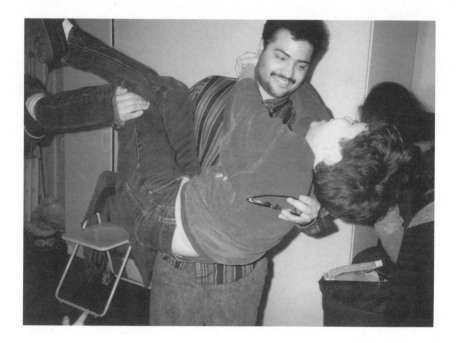

Aurelio and Bret
(Photo by Marion Cohen)

56

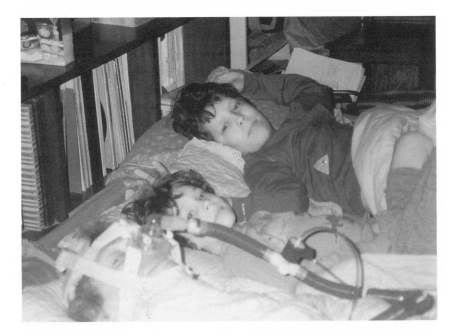

"The family respirator": Jeff, Devin, and Bret
(Photo by Marion Cohen)

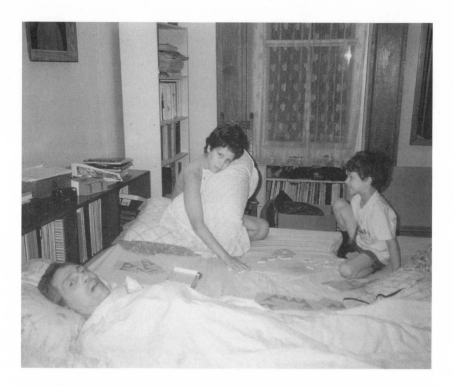

"The family bed": Jeff, Bret, and Devin
(Photo by Marion Cohen)

A family birthday party: Bret, Jeff, Devin, and Arin
(Photo by Marion Cohen)

59

*Writing: often Jeff was in the hospital bed two feet away
(Photo by Anna Kaufman Moon)*

More family bed: Jeff, Devin, and I
(Photo by Anna Kaufman Moon)

61

Emptying the catheter bag
(Photo by Anna Kaufman Moon)

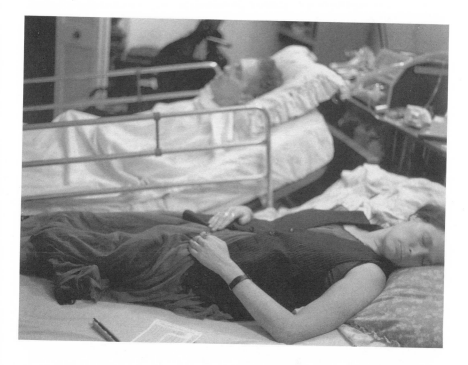

After introducing the hospital bed, a rare moment of sleep
(Photo by Anna Kaufman Moon)

63

Jeff and I
(Photo by Anna Kaufman Moon)

64

Supper time
(Photo by Anna Kaufman Moon)

65

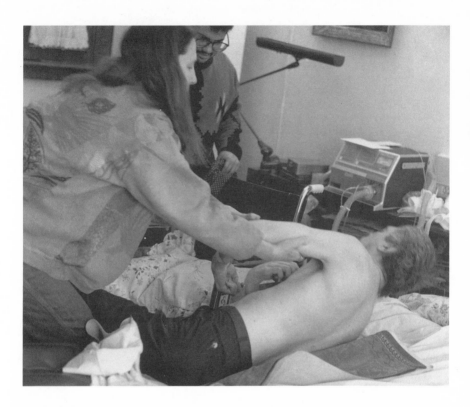

Getting Jeff up in the morning
(Photo by Anna Kaufman Moon)

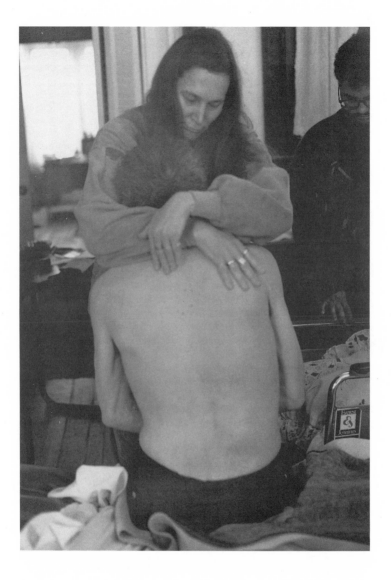

Catching my breath between steps two and three of getting Jeff
out of bed: a worried moment
(Photo by Anna Kaufman Moon)

With my wonderful social worker daughter
(Photo by Anna Kaufman Moon)

Phyllis and I singing Mozart and Verdi operas in my living room, often interrupted by calls of "Mar!" and "Toilet!" (Photo by Anna Kaufman Moon)

69

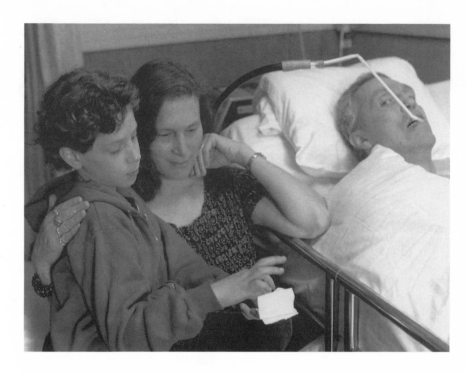

*Devin and I visiting Jeff at Inglis House
(Photo by Anna Kaufman Moon)*

scared
four

I was scared. Scared about specifics, like what if Jeff fell on the floor and there were no attendants around to help get him back up (something that actually happened several times)? And scared in general—the kind of scared when you've just started a new job or had a new baby, and you don't quite know what you're scared of.

"You're one body in charge of moving two bodies," Bret would say at age about eleven.

"It didn't feel secure," our daughter, Marielle remembers now at twenty-four. "We could never plan anything. There were so many factors that could go wrong. Everything would be all set—like, we'd be about to go out somewhere—and then suddenly Dad would have to go to the bathroom."

At one of the well-spouse annual conventions there were separate workshops for men and women. At the women's workshop we talked about fear of poverty, fear of being left with no income or social security. "And," I added, "there's something else I feel, and that's fear of something even worse than poverty. I'm not even sure how to describe it; I think it's fear of being, not even homeless, but streetless.

71

It's fear of being in a situation where you don't know what to do—of being a street person without a street, or something." I hadn't known how to describe it, but now I heard a few soft voices whispering yes and I felt the entire room nod.

And suppose there was a fire, or a burglar? Suppose the Gulf War got to the United States? Not only couldn't Jeff protect us but we'd have to get him out of the house. In a hurry. He weighed 155 pounds. What if there were an explosion and Jeff and I were the only ones left in the world—no attendants, at all, ever?

Once we discovered a rat in the house. It was too late in the evening to call an exterminator. Besides, it was Memorial Day. We couldn't even stay overnight at any friend's house because all the houses in this neighborhood have front steps, and no ramps. I did locate an exterminator that evening, but we were left feeling humbled.

Sometimes we'd be home alone, the kids all out with friends or asleep. The electric clock would be ticking. "That means it's starting to go," Jeff would remark. It seemed all our possessions were starting to go. Dishwasher, VCR, even the living-room Oriental rug had an unexplained crevice toward the southwest corner. Because of finances, or our worry about finances, we never replaced anything. We were phasing everything out, maybe even ourselves.

So scary, so undependable, was our house that once Marielle reached college age, she chose not to live in it, even though it was only a mile from the college.

One of the things that helped me through being scared was having Devin. A week after he was born Arin, then twelve, looked at me in wonder and remarked, "Mom, you're glowing." I kept glowing for seven years, even through nights, lifting, and toilet. Still, I was scared. You can glow and be scared at the same time.

"*More* scared," I kept writing in my diary. Scared like Bret's hamster lost in our wall. Scared about bills in the mail, like that erroneous one for fifteen thousand and something from the City of Philadelphia. Scared when Jeff said we couldn't keep our Oriental rug on the first floor if we got a kitten and we'd already promised one to Bret. Scared about the huge trike on the first floor that Jeff got from a friend and that he couldn't possibly use, a gigantic child's tricycle, maybe four feet all around that he said he'd take to his office at Penn; but I didn't need one more big thing I couldn't move, didn't need one more body to be in charge of. Scared that none of the four attendants we'd be interviewing that week would work out.

Of course, I was scared of letting strangers into our home all the time. As it turned out, nothing bad ever happened; we never got robbed, I never got raped or even had to fend off a pass, but weird stuff went on, and our home was wide open. One morning Patty, a new attendant, showed up at 6:40 A.M., instead of the agreed upon and usual 9:00. There was no denying *that* discrepancy. Since we hadn't said anything when she arrived an hour early for the evening job of putting Jeff to bed (she and the kids liked to play together), she must have felt it was okay to arrive early in the morning also.

I'd sensed something needy about Patty; she'd been too attentive, for example, always bringing us flowers (which we suspected were picked from people's front-yard gardens) and thrift-shop stuff for me, always telling us how much she liked us. She'd been forcing the friendship, and much too fast. She wasn't the only attendant who had what my therapist called problems with boundaries. Arriving on our doorstep at 6:40 was ridiculous and I told her if she ever did anything like that again she was out. If she'd been a baby-sitter (a lot easier to come by), she'd have been out then and there.

One morning a week later I awoke to Jeff needing a jar. That was no news, nor was the bedpan immediately afterwards; what was news was that the doorbell rang. It seemed darkish outside; I glanced at the clock. "Oh, no," I groaned. "Not Patty again. And it's not even 7:30." I checked the window mirror and yes, Patty. I decided to just let the doorbell ring. "I told her," I kept muttering. "I know I told her." And then, "Well, as far as she knows, we're sleeping. And I don't care if she leaves and doesn't come back. After all, this is our home."

After the second ring she stopped and sat down on our front steps. I lay awake. Fifteen, twenty minutes later she rang again. I still didn't answer. "I definitely told her. There's no way she couldn't have understood." She sat on our steps until 7:55 and then tried again. I finally let her in. I had said I didn't care if she left and never came back, but of course I did. It was a matter of my life. But I definitely told her "definitely" again.

In general, I was scared of the attendants—scared they wouldn't show and scared they would. I was scared of my own home. In those years there seemed to be a spate of TV specials on typical middle-class family descends into home-lessness. I always felt in danger of homelessness. One of the things necessary to our home was attendants, and it seemed we were going to have to spend the rest of our lives looking for them or being afraid every morning they wouldn't show. When they were around, it wasn't home either, not our own home. I often felt as though we were already homeless.

Yet there we still were, the three boys watching TV together, or happily eating their favorites in the kitchen—Arin a frozen Salisbury steak dinner, Bret leftover spaghetti and sauce, and Devin "some of Mommy's," usually salad, on Mommy's lap. We were not homeless, and we had a very wonderful home. We empowered ourselves in many ways. But we were also depowered in many ways. And we were still scared.

The kids were scared, too. Or I'd worry that they were. When we were out together Dev would often say things like "I wanna go home" and "Our house is far away." One evening I took him to the square and on the walk over he stopped and told me, "I don't want to go." So we turned around and went back home. "Is this ages-and-stages stuff?" I'd wonder. "Or is it like Paula?" Paula was one of my childhood friends from the neighborhood. One summer she suddenly started wanting to go home all the time and wasn't any fun to play with. After a while my mother told me that Paula's father was having a drinking problem and that her mother was considering leaving him. Paula was worried about her home, my mother explained, so she was always wanting to go back there and check up on things. "Is that what Dev's going through?" I'd worry.

We would fight fear with love. Out in the streets, all of us, right in the middle of Chestnut Street, Dev would tug at my blouse. "Not *here*," Bret would say, but yes, here. Discreetly, to be sure, but here, there, anywhere. When you're in dire straits, or even when you're not, the thing to do is to admit when you're scared and to be comforted.

If it was a scary home, it was also loving. Jeff's illness meant we were together more; we often had to be. Sometimes we resented it, but what I remember is lounging on the big bed—Jeff, me, and the two youngest. I remember reading or drawing with Bret while nursing Dev. I remember Jeff helping Bret with physics. Or all of us parallel playing or parallel working—Bret drawing, Dev playing UNO or Lego, Jeff doing physics, me writing. We also spent some nights together on that big bed; that is, we had what's known as "the family bed," all of us sleeping together. We handled the fear and the anger and the sadness and the dire straits with love. I was articulate about the fear and anger and about the dire straits, and I was articulate about the love.

So I was a far cry from being alone and from being lonely, but fear of loneliness was something to contend with. I'd dream of flying in the vast night sky. I was a bird. Space was very dark, but some portions were darker than others. I kept weaving in and out of those darker spots, so lonely.

Or I'd dream of being abandoned. In my parents' old house—they were there, alive again, but neither happy nor supportive—my father stood at my left, and not close, my mother at my right, even farther away. I was lying on the cold hard floor, not even a rug, having a baby. I also had some disability and couldn't get up or put my arms in front of me. "The baby's coming," I exclaimed and, expertly, happily, I let it come. Well, half-happily, for my father and mother were doing nothing to help. "It's a girl," I exclaimed, but no one exclaimed with me. I wriggled around and reached on either side, grabbed the baby as best I could, began to hold and nurse her. There were no blankets for either of us.

That dream was not fear, it only smacked of fear. It was only nightmarish. During a nightmare you don't always realize it's a nightmare, and your heart doesn't always pound. That's what our house was like, a lot of the time. Things only smacked of fear, only felt nightmarish.

During the broken-ankle era I would think, "Suppose there's a reason I broke a bone just from falling? Suppose my bones are too soft? Suppose there's something more to it than a simple break? And you know how I'm always saying that *Jeff* has no choice; he has to live this way, but that I have a choice? Suppose that's no longer true? Suppose I had my chance? And suppose I never walk again? Suppose, soon, it's attendant care for me, too?" And the lump of fear would grow as I thought of the kids.

In the bath I'd stare at my arm and say, aloud, "I can't die when I have such a nice sunburn."

"I can't die when I'm still breast-feeding." "I can't die if I just had a baby." "I can't die while I'm thrift shopping." I alternated fear with reassurance. People who live with fear have to do that. But the very reassurances feel nightmarish, and of course I knew I could die. You can drop dead any-where, even in a thrift shop. You can die in childbirth. You can get breast cancer, sunstroke.

Naturally I thought about death more than I would have had Jeff not been so sick and disabled. Who, for example, is going to hold my hand when I'm dying? Everyone will be dead themselves or used up by Jeff. The kids were also thinking about death more than they would have, or I'd worry that they were. Watching a scary TV movie with Devin, I'd cuddle him and say, "But none of that's going to happen to you."

"Uh-huh," he'd counter. "What about a long time from now when I don't look like I do now?" Sickness and death, in our house, were highly apparent. ■

Sometimes fear would turn to horror. One evening I was so, so tired. I had a cold, with a clogged ear; I had lain down all afternoon, worrying and feeling guilty about the kids. Bret came over and said, "I'm staying with Dad tonight. He and I decided."

"Thanks," I said. "You know, it's wonderful to have a kid like you." I hugged him as much as the August heat would allow.

We all stayed in the family bed for a while and watched a rerun, then I went into a separate room to get in a lot of good solid hours of sleep. I lay awake, beginning to relax, think-ing how lucky I was to have a kid like Bret, and how nice it was that Jeff, this time, had noticed how tired I was and had taken it upon himself to suggest Bret do this night. My ear was feeling better as I drifted off.

Suddenly Bret was tapping me. "Mom, Dad's too heavy for me to roll over." That was horror, "existential horror," it's called. You know how it is when you wake up—suddenly things exist. Suddenly you exist. And your unwell spouse exists. You had forgotten about it all.

Sometimes it was a matter of psychological horror, the kind Hitchcock made movies about. A year or so ago, when I had decided that Jeff had to live in a nursing home, he was on steroids and had been acting a little scary, his voice stronger and more demanding, his words strangely euphoric, even more denying and unrealistic than usual. My friend Freda, my oldest and dearest, was visiting from Staten Island. Jeff was upstairs with one of the kids; Freda and I were downstairs making a spaghetti dinner, relaxing and laughing, when I heard a partly familiar voice from upstairs. "I'm not going into any nursing home. You're not going to put me in a nursing home."

I went upstairs, and Jeff said other ugly things, like "If you want to get rid of me, you leave. I'm not going to leave."

What was so horrifying to me was his power to keep hurting us. I'd always assumed it was my choice that he live at home. Now I saw that maybe it wasn't. Or soon wouldn't be.

"Oh my god," I thought, "I'm afraid of him. He can hurt us, he may hurt us, he's allowed to hurt us." He was a stranger in the house holding us at gunpoint. If I said the wrong thing he'd shoot.

That, to me, was well-spouse fear at its peak. Many similar incidents followed, and for a while the atmosphere in our household—and, later, in the hospital—was full of his outbursts, fear, and distrust. But that, thank goodness, was the peak.

And I have been lucky. Jeff has not been actually abusive. Not all well spouses can say the same. Deborah Hayden's "Forum" in a recent well-spouse newsletter (entitled *Mainstay* after Maggie Strong's book) is on violence. Here are two anonymous excerpts: "A very serious disability didn't put an end to my spouse's physical and emotional abuse. After his accident, a spinal cord injury which paralyzed him from the neck down, he just needed to find new ways to carry out the desperate need to control through violence. I believe nothing will stop the more determined abusers." And the second: "He has made his power wheelchair his main weapon. I have scars on my legs and ankles to prove it! He has bitten me, spit on me, and even poked me in the face with a little metal clip he has attached to an arm and hand brace to hold his cigarettes. When I'm caring for him, I'm close enough for a surprise attack." ■

What am I scared or horrified of now? The financial arrangements haven't been settled yet. Jeff's insurance is paying for Inglis House, but we don't know for how long. It takes insurance companies a long time to determine things like that. We might have to go on medical assistance. This morning my well-spouse friend Norma, whose husband had a stroke and has been in a nursing home four years, spent as many hours on the phone dealing with red tape concerning her medical assistance. "It's been horrendous," she says. She has also been getting threatening phone calls at least once a day and is becoming afraid to live alone.

In general, I'm scared of the future. I don't know to what extent I'm still a wife, to what extent I want to be. I've given myself permission to fall in love with someone else, or to be attracted to someone else and to act on that attraction, but I'm not the slightest bit interested. I do understand that I need the space, that I need to be alone, but I still worry about whether there's something wrong with me. In the same way that when we first got married it felt strange to know that people knew we were having sex, now it feels strange, with Jeff at Inglis House, to think that people know we're not having sex. Strange and scary.

My fear of death and of growing old is escalating more than it would be, I believe, if I were fifty-one and not a well spouse. I'm scared of not looking good in long hair and long dresses, and I'm scared of Altzheimer's. I also worry about the time that has elapsed since the births of my children, that I'll forget the births, or that the memories will become like childhood memories, far too dim. I'm scared that, when I'm dead, I'll still be conscious; in particular, I'm scared I'll feel the need to breathe.

But most of all I'm scared Inglis House will send Jeff back. Either by mistake or because both medical assistance and Blue Cross will refuse to pay. Even though nursing homes are not allowed to do that, I know two well spouses whose ill spouses were "kicked out" because they were demented or disturbed and touched or attacked other patients. The way the nursing homes get around the law is to send the patient to a hospital, then refuse to take him back—that they're allowed to do.

I'm scared Jeff will change his mind and suddenly appear,

Kafka style, on my doorstep or in my bed. Or on the toilet. Or on the trike calling "Toilet."

Norma and I often joke about that fear. We can always count on each other if we need someone to laugh away our fears with. It's funny-familiar, not funny ha-ha. "Jeff keeps talking about how he expects to get better," I say.

"Bite your tongue," interjects Norma, in stereotypical Jewish dialect, and we burst out laughing.

"Cause we know that means partially better—right?"

"Right." We pause. "Just better enough to come home." We laugh knowingly.

"Bite your tongue," I go, and we laugh some more.

She tells me of an incident just this past week. She had spotted an item in the Einstein Hospital news bulletin, "Give Stroke Victims a Second Chance," advocating physical therapy even after years of no apparent progress, even after giving up. Norma had shown that article to the staff at her husband's nursing home and they had decided to give him that second chance. He had begun walking a little, not much, maybe half a step. Norma had asked one of the guys on the physical-therapy staff, "So what's the bottom line here?"

"Well," the guy had answered, "he'll never be a functional walker. The most he'll ever do is be able to help the aides help him."

And it had just come out, though softly, before Norma had time to control herself. "Whew!"

The guy and she had laughed together; he had put his arm around her shoulder and given it a little squeeze, as if to say, "Yes, I know you've had it." He had understood.

Sometimes I think I wouldn't even want Jeff to get completely better. It would complicate my life; I would suspect him of only pretending to be better, or only temporarily better; as soon as we severed all connections with the nursing home, as soon as we threw out our list of resources (bite your tongue), he'd have a relapse.

A few nights ago I had my first Jeff-coming-home dream. (I had expected to dream that sooner.) Years ago, at a well-spouse convention, a well spouse with a husband in a nursing home had said to me, "I do like it when he comes home for Thanksgiving, but it makes me nervous." In my dream Jeff came home for Thanksgiving and announced that he was staying. He had that same look on his face he had last year when he boomed, "I'm not going into any nursing home," and that same look he gets now when I visit him and he complains to me about, say, the aides not answering the call bell fast enough. That look is hard, steadfast, and seems to say, "It's your fault" or "What are you going to do about it?"

In the dream he said to me, half assuringly, half bitterly and accusingly, "You don't have to take care of me. I'll just call up Jackie, or Colleen, or Patty . . . "

Patty of 6:30 A.M? Jackie and Colleen who had long since burned out?

Yes, I'm scared he'll come back. Scared I'll have to do nights, lifting, and toilet again. Scared that, suddenly in the night, he'll be inexplicably at my side, calling "Mar!" and "Toilet!"

The kids are scared of that, too. A couple of weeks after Jeff wasn't living at home any more, the bell rang and

Benny, the attendant, came in to pick up his last check. The kids were in the living room and I joked to them, "Don't worry—Dad's not with him!" We all laughed; we all understood. Benny, too. We're getting that fear under control, and humor is one of our strategies.

Every once in a while, though, an Inglis House resident other than Jeff asks me for something. Gary wanted me to take off his shirt. Some guy in North Solarium wanted me to help him light a cigarette; I don't smoke so I'm not great at cigarette lighting; moreover, his lighter didn't seem to be working. He had that same matter-of-fact repeating-the-demand voice that Jeff has. And by the elevator, a woman whose mind must be a bit off calls in a high-pitched voice, "Lady. Lady." She has that same look that I know so well in Jeff.

If they knew my name was Mar, they'd call "Mar!" I feel like saying, "I'm out of the Mar business." I also recall those Resources for Living Independently lists of four attendants at a time; none of those names on any of those lists ever amounted to anything. Some were characters, but most would say, when we called, "Oh, I don't do that kind of work any more." I feel like saying, "I don't do that kind of work any more." In fact, I feel like calling Resources for Living Independently and everybody else and telling them, "Get me off the list."

I think of Jeff's mother, visiting his father at rehab after his stroke. She was feeding the other patients in the room, buttoning and pulling off shirts. That's her way, and it's not mine. Thinking of her doing those things, I recoil. I can't bear to think of being like that. I don't mind helping out with Jeff—in fact, it sometimes gives me great pleasure, to be helping instead of helped—but the idea of being "Mar" to the other residents gets me pretty nervous. I need to be off that list but good.

Every once in a while, Benny stops by—"Just to say hello," he says. A little too friendly and maybe a little high on something, he walks in and assumes he's welcome here anytime, assumes he still works here, assumes this is his house in the way it used to be when he was Jeff's attendant. The last time this happened, Aurelio and I held a small spur-of-the-moment conference in the kitchen in which we decided to tell the kids, "Next time Benny comes, tell him we're busy now; this isn't a good time."

But it feels unnerving, if not scary. Maybe all the attendants, all those characters, will start paying us visits. Maybe Patty at 6:30, or 5:30 A.M. Or maybe William; maybe the service will forget we no longer use it and send William, talking to himself, mimicking Jeff's nicknames for me. Maybe we haven't gotten rid of them, after all. Jeff's out of the house for good, but maybe not all those characters.

We're still scared. Only occasionally, and nothing like before. But still just a little scared. ■

too many variables:
relationships within the household
five

What happens to love when the lovers are forced together, in close quarters like a bathroom, or a toilet? What happens to love if the lovers are Siamese twins? Or when one of the lovers is a Siamese twin—with his attendant? What happens when one of the lovers is, in twelve-year-old Bret's words, in charge of both bodies? If the two of you were the only ones left in the world, what would happen to love, even without that one-sided dependency? What happens to love during just plain hard times, temporary hard times, when things are simply not going well?

Jeff and I kept our love life and our sex life throughout most of what we've gone through, both the ordinary stress and the dire straits. We even chose, nine years ago, when he was already a wheelchair user, to have another baby. We probably never stopped communicating; certainly I said what was on my mind, and I tried to say what was on his. He was less articulate, more of a denier. I would try to get him to stop denying, not only for his sake but also because the denial was often too much for me. Or it would hurt me. If, for example, he denied that he was having more and more trouble turning over in bed, that meant the difficulties in turning him were my fault. It also meant that those difficulties went unacknowledged. So, sometimes gently, sometimes angrily, I fought his denial by trying to get him to say, and usually eventually myself saying, what was on his mind, or what I thought should be on his mind.

People have said, "It's amazing, how you kept on going. Such a terrible thing happened and you just kept on going." For a long time we provided a life and a home for ourselves, our kids, and our cats. More and more, however, I felt less compassionate toward Jeff, less able to love him strongly, to say a long tender good-bye to the love of my life, and to mourn the gradual losing of him and the anticipated sudden loss of him. I was too busy doing nights, lifting, and toilet, or worrying or tantruming about them. I was also busy sorting things out, protecting the me in me (finding time and space for writing, teaching, thrift shopping, singing) and protecting the mother in me, for the sake of both the kids and me.

I was, in short, fighting for my life. I once spoke with a mother who lost a baby in the second trimester. "As soon as I started hemmorhaging," she told me, "the focus immediately switched from saving the baby to saving me." That's what was happening to my focus. It was pure survival instinct.

Jeff was aware of all this, because I told him, many times. He would nod. I hoped that meant he understood that, eventually, he would have to be in a nursing home. But I see now that he was probably caught up in his own survival instinct—to stay home with his family, to keep his life, the him in him.

I'm not fighting for my life now. And he, for the most part, has accepted what is happening, if not what is going to happen. And even as his condition advances, his voice weakens, and we worry about money, our relationship can proceed . . . well, to its natural conclusion. I can begin to feel the loss, both the present loss and the future loss, and I can begin to say good-bye. We can begin to say good-bye. ∎

In an early poem I wrote that Jeff and I were "becoming separate species"; that poem is a favorite among well spouses. At the time that I wrote it, only his diet and sleep habits were separate. Over the years the separation grew. There were nights when Bret or Aurelio or Beverly would be "on" with him, and we would be in separate bedrooms. The mornings after those nights I'd find that I liked to get dressed, washed, teeth brushed, breakfast made, and any other chores done first, before my final chore of going downstairs to say good morning to Jeff.

For that was a chore. Not only because he might need jar or bedpan or phone call, but also because we were "becoming separate species" more and more. And you have to make special efforts to visit someone of a separate species. Now he's even more separate. Now I literally visit him.

As long as Jeff lived with us, I was unable to look at or be with him without expecting him, any second, to call "Mar!" *Controlling* was the word used by Bobbi, a well-spouse friend who has formed Age-Wise, a social service specifically for family members of sick and dying people. Jeff controlled when we could go out in the morning, what time we went to bed in the evening, whether we got sleep at night, and whether during the day we could have an uninterrupted game of Scrabble. The entire household revolved around him.

I'd be in Marielle's room, for instance, curled up in her bed. Out of sight, but not out of mind. The awayness was an illusion. He was in the next room, propped up with a jar. Soon he'd be calling "Mar!" Right now he was probably refraining from calling "Mar!" So controlling, whether he wanted to be or not.

But by and large, we had to get out of the house to relax, the opposite of the way it is with most families, who do their relaxing at home. We sometimes went out for dinner, when it seemed worth the hassle and the worry that Jeff would have to toilet without a toilet. But when we got back, I'd still have not slept the previous night and I'd sit down and fall across the kitchen table, only to be awakened five minutes later by "Mar, I think I need to sit on the toilet" and then "I waited an hour to ask you." When I would literally cry from fatigue, he would say, "If you get me all upset, I won't be able to go." *Controlling* was the word.

In the middle of the night, Jeff would say, "Raise the ankle." "It's not *the* ankle," I'd grunt. "It's *an* ankle. Do you think you own the only ankle? What about *my* ankle? The one I broke last year?"

Ultimately, we communicated. We communicated well. His denial met my anger, my heightened acceptance. The first time he couldn't press the stairglide button, I had to follow him up the stairs, hold him with my arms, and push the button with my elbow, something like that. "This is ridiculous," I kept saying.

He shrugged. "I'm in bad shape today."

That pushed *my* button. "Jeff." I sighed loudly. "I can't relate to you when you deny like that. What do you mean, today? Can't you call a spade a spade?"

So that time he did call a spade a spade; he quietly conceded, "Mar, I don't know if the niacin'll work or not. I just plan to try it and hope it does. I haven't been doing too well lately and I just hope I get better again. We'll have to wait and see."

I couldn't relate to that, either. I needed him to deny, I realized. Or I liked it; a part of me liked it. I don't think I enabled or encouraged him to deny, but I did, sometimes, like and need it. So I nodded and made a compassionate face, but I couldn't bring myself to hug him or hold him. That, at the time, seemed like admitting, like accepting, like somehow cooperating, like giving his disease, and our dire straits, my blessing. I couldn't touch him. I had to deny him, too.

Other times I did hold him. Plenty of times. I also told him about my own brand of denial, and that it sometimes met his brand. Sometimes our communication got very positive. An article on the first page of the *Philadelphia Inquirer* told of another possible but not probable cure for MS. They'd isolated an MS virus. "In humans?" we asked. Yes, in humans. Jeff was excited; I surprised myself by being a little excited, too, all set to pretend, all set to fantasize, all set to join Jeff in positive visualization. After all we'd gone through, all the anger and failure, at times, to love properly, after so many years of strengthening my survival instinct, I was ready to fall in love again. "We'll go tripping together through the thrift shops," I sang. "We'll go to plays, restaurants; we'll take walks in the park."

He nodded significantly. "And we'll go dancing."

I was amazed at how easily we could forget—and forgive—the MS.

Sometimes I was wise. Jeff would deny, and I'd smirk and shrug instead of tantrum. "Look what I can do," he'd tell me. "I couldn't do this before my juice fast." And he'd lean all the way forward in the trike, head to his knees, then push back up. "I wouldn't try this if you weren't in the room," he'd add. "I'd be worried that I'd get stuck."

He'd begin leaning forward again and I'd smirk to myself, knowing what was coming. It came even sooner than I'd expected. "Ooops! I'm stuck. Mar, could you . . . ?" I'd smirk again, only slightly pleased at my wisdom. But now, as I write, I see that denial can be a way of expressing something, that perhaps Jeff's way of showing me the limited effectiveness of his juice fast and his feelings about it was, though indirect, more accurate.

We communicated. We acknowledged our situation; it was our life together. Sometimes, in quiet moments, we could be like an older couple, sitting back and basking in it all, perhaps reminiscing. One July both our older kids were away; Arin, then eighteen, was using part of his savings to fly to Colorado campsites, then on to Jamaica. Marielle was in California, celebrating her graduation from college, trying out new health-food restaurants and thrift stores.

Jeff tapped me and said, "We had all that, too, a long time ago."

Memories help, good romantic memories. But there are limitations to memories. For there are also bad memories. That's normal and natural and okay; what's not so great is that the bad memories seem to connect up with the present dire straits. The escalation of our dire straits offset much of the progress we made in therapy. One of our issues was Jeff's tendency to need to be taken care of emotionally. Once, at the pool when he was about six, his father called, "Jump, I'll catch you." Jeff did, and his father didn't. So on dates he'd ask me, "Where should we go?" and then, in the restaurant, "What should I order?" Or he'd need me to type his physics papers and it was not, in his case, a feminist issue. I made progress with respect to not always complying with his needs, but he didn't make much progress, and with MS that kind of progress became next to impossible for him, because feeling safe and being taken care of were needs only height-ened by his illness. I became highly frustrated when Jeff hired a bad attendant and took forever to fire him, or when he got the service's forms mixed up, causing us a lot of grief. He didn't, to me, seem quite as upset about toilet as he should have been. "By George," I'd sometimes think, "he *likes* toilet. He likes being toileted." My therapist told me I expected too much. That is, my baggage got into it, too.

What I'm saying is that memories are not always the answer. Reminiscing can bring on bitterness. Thinking about good memories can remind you of the bad, and the dire straits can give the bad memories more weight.

Indeed, at well-spouse meetings people have described

their ill spouses' self-centeredness, or demandingness, or verbal abusiveness and then reminisced about the same qualities in their spouse before the illness. "He'd be that way," they've concluded, "even if he hadn't got sick." ∎

Jeff and I communicated about the sadness and irony. When most of his friends or colleagues, even his brother, visited him and he had to jar, he'd send them out to get me. "Mar!" they'd call. Sometimes he did that because the visitor refused to do jar, and sometimes it was because Jeff wouldn't even tell the visitor he needed jar; he'd just ask the visitor to go get Mar. I confronted Jeff about this, and I got an honest answer: "I'm afraid if I ask them, they'll stop visiting."

I felt for him, but I had another question: "Aren't you afraid I'll stop visiting?"

We also communicated about the politics of illness and disaster. Getting upset about politics was probably Jeff's brand of anger, and we very definitely got upset together; thinking and analyzing with emotion were our strengths. We once watched a thirty-minute infomercial that first showed a "devoted grandmother" who'd almost lost her granddaughter because she hadn't known CPR, then a mother whose toddler son almost drowned in the family pool but "if I'd only known CPR there wouldn't have been brain damage." Then we learned that for "only" $79.95 we could buy a tape that would teach us CPR. "Why don't they just use the thirty minutes to teach us now?" I asked, and Jeff nodded.

"The most important member of the medical team," the program told us, "is you."

"Then why don't they pay me?" I quipped.

"Because," Jeff answered, "they know you'll do it for free."

"Yes," I added, "just like the service wouldn't pay me if I were to decide to be your full-time attendant." We both smirked; that, we knew, would be the last thing I'd decide.

"Even," I continued, "if neither they nor we nor anyone else could find another full-time attendant. They know I'd have to do it. I'd rush to do it. I'd beg to do it. Otherwise, they know that I know the mess I'd be left with." Yes, we were on the same wavelength when it came to that kind of thing. ■

Three or four years ago Roberta, my publisher and friend, said, "One thing you haven't expressed, and that's Why doesn't he just die already?" Indeed, it was several years before I felt anything approaching that, and even then I felt that maybe I wanted him to die but not now, not yet; please, not yet.

I wrote a poem, "That Room," about our bedroom, where, beginning two or three years ago, Jeff sat in the trike almost all day, the room from whence "Mar!" issued. I didn't want to be there, and I got out of there whenever I could, but when something bad happened to me, or something good, I'd go zooming right back in. Jeff was the one I wanted to tell, especially if it was a math problem or solution, or some incident with my calculus students. And he was the one who would say, "You're great, Mar," or "Don't worry, Mar"—just as he had when I was laboring with each of the babies.

It's still that way, to some extent. Only now that room is a couple of miles away. Instead of going into that room, I call it up. I am getting more and more ready, sometimes willing, even anxious, for Jeff to die, but I do like having that room.

The two of us have talked about most of this—more acknowledging, and more completing our life together in what I believe is style. Two birthdays ago, when Jeff was turning fifty-one, the evening felt depressing. The day had been good; the kids had made Jeff a special breakfast (blended figs, bananas, whatever his thing was at the time) and we'd had a special dinner, either raw veggies or curried cabbage and potatoes and carrot cake, a cake-shaped mound of grated carrots with a sagging candle in the middle.

But I had fed Jeff and later brushed his teeth; that had become pretty much the story in those days. We were feeling sad, especially since he soon needed toilet. So we sat— he on the toilet, me at the toilet. Or I might have been sitting out in the hallway on the stairglide, as we lamented together. "We're far too stressed. Far, far too frightened, and far, far too angry. I guess we're going to be not being very nice to each other. And the number of times, the frequency, that we're not very nice to each other is going to go up and up."

"Our romance won't end well," I added. He nodded.

"It began very well, but it won't end well." He nodded again. ■

Time and energy given the unwell spouse subtracts from time and energy given everyone else in the household. And those others might be hurt or angry, especially in cases like ours, where those others are children.

I was determined to have a "continuum" relationship with the baby, which meant wearing him almost twenty-four hours a day, breast-feeding on demand, having him in the bed at night. Both Jeff and I wanted things with our last child to be that way; we wanted it not only for Devin's sake, but for ours. Before Devin reached the crawling stage, Jeff only needed people to bring him things from across the room or to write things down for him; he used the trike but was almost completely independent. So my relationship with the baby was not threatened by the MS, and it was wonderful.

I like to think that, because I'm expressive and communicative, my relationships with the other three kids have also not suffered. Indeed, all of them seem to have adjusted quite well to their father's being in a nursing home. Basically, we all share the euphoria of freedom. Jeff and I discussed the decision with them every step of the way, shared feelings—sadness, possible guilt, sympathy with their dad—and mostly, how good it feels to sit around the table and not hear "Mar!"

For Jeff and me, having the kids around made MS and my being a well spouse more palatable, sometimes even fun. I remember especially Devin and kittens swinging in the Hoyer lift. This device consisted of a canvas "swing" attached to a metal frame. When Jeff needed to be moved, the attendant would roll him into the swing, where he would sit as the mechanism hoisted him over the floor. In time, it became just another piece of furniture in our bedroom, and occasionally it served double duty as playground equipment for Dev and the kittens.

But what about the kids' point of view?

Marielle is our oldest. During my pregnancy twenty-four years ago we nicknamed her Elle so she wouldn't be called "Mar," like me. Elle's the only one who had at least part of a childhood without MS; in fact, she was eighteen and away at college, although in the same city, when the dire straits began, a young adult rather than a child during those years. Mature in other ways and ever the future social worker, she has almost never failed to be compassionate and helpful—and quick to worry. When she came home from college to visit, she came, I realized, not only to see us and the doings of her toddler brother, but also because she needed to make sure things were okay.

I also remember being dimly aware, during toilet, of happy sounds coming from downstairs in the kitchen, or upstairs in Bret's room, where Marielle was doting on the younger kids, trying to help make this a reasonable home for them ("normal," as she now puts it). We were concerned that too much was being asked of her, that she was asking too much of herself. And to me, privately, she would say, "I know I'm a worrier. I feel as if Daddy made me that way." She was also, increasingly, someone with whom I could talk about my own worries and frustration. In the last few years Jeff was at home, she initiated conversations with both of us about nursing homes, calmly pointing out to her dad how his care was getting too complicated to be done at home.

Arin, now just twenty-one, was probably the child most hurt by MS; he was four when Jeff was diagnosed and until he was nine lived with a father obviously sick but choosing not to tell anybody except his wife what he was sick with. (In the same season that Jeff was diagnosed, our family lost Arin's newborn sister.) Arin kept saying, early on, "Daddy should be in a hospital or something" and now says, "People who can't take care of themselves should be put out on the streets and just left there. I don't actually mean that. I just mean I feel that way." On the other hand, he has also remarked, "We have all kinds of other interesting things around our house—we might as well have a disabled person!"

Born sixteen months after the baby who died, Bret, at fifteen, is a little like Elle. He's helpful and compassionate, especially toward me; he did two nights a week beginning at age ten but burned out entirely and suddenly at age twelve; he still needs to be reassured that we weren't mad at him for that.

All three of the older kids make it a point to visit Jeff regularly, if not frequently, and to include him in their lives as much as is realistically possible. Arin, for example, calls him up if he has a question about any of his college classes, and Bret enlists his aid in science papers and projects.

Devin, the youngest, never really bonded with his father, who has been increasingly too self-absorbed to bond in any big way. When Dev was very little, Jeff took him outside for rides in the trike, but now the two rarely hug or touch.

I like to think that my relationships with the kids have

been intact all along. I like to think there were only occasional sad incidents, when the dire straits we all were in alienated us from each other—or alienated them. After one of my tantrums, I noticed Bret looking hurt. I went over to him and quietly said, "It's not my job to hide what I'm feeling. And it's not your job to hide what you're feeling." But Bret had already started sadly up the stairs.

When I had finished feeding Jeff, I went upstairs to Bret. "We should talk about our feelings," I said. "Our family has a very terrible situation and most of the time we all just laugh with and love each other and have a good time together but sometimes we get frustrated and we have to say what we're feeling."

But Bret only said, "It hurts my mind."

And then my mind hurt, so I changed the subject. But all the while I felt like the human wives among the Stepford women just before they're killed by their look-alike replacements, as they realize they're about to be replaced as mothers, too. Would Bret prefer I be a Stepford wife, a robot who would do nights, lifting, and toilet without tantruming, without minding, without having a mind?

Dire straits made me more sensitive to the kids' needs and beauties, especially the baby's. "When I grow up," Dev would ask, "will I still eat on you?"

"You won't want to," I answered, only a little sadly. "You'll be big, as big as me, probably bigger, and you'll have a wife or a lover and maybe babies, and you just won't want to."

Devin sported that incredible knows-he's-sweet expression and said, "Yes I will."

My eyes welled up with love and I kept silent. When I spoke again, I was staring straight ahead. "You're going to be a wonderful husband and father," I said. "Stay just the way you are. Stay just as sweet and as lovely as you are. Don't get all worried and nervous and inhibited and turn out to have MS and make your wife put you on the toilet . . . " By now, my saying had turned to whispering, and my whispering to thinking. And to crying. And Devin was comforting me.

Marielle nurtured me, too. Once after she took me out for my birthday, as she did every year, we called home to see if Bret and Devin wanted to meet us in the park. On the phone I could tell immediately that something was wrong. Finally Bret said, "Patty went crazy again, and she ran off with Dad's check; she said Dad owed her money. She just ran out so fast nobody could stop her or say anything to her."

This was during Benny's "halo period," and we knew we were not going to find another attendant. We rushed home right away—no park, no more birthday dinner or dessert. That day home to me felt like a black hole—no choice but to go in, no way to get out.

Once we got home amidst all the commotion, explanations, and lamenting, Marielle set about straightening up and cleaning the kitchen counter, a calm but determined expression on her face. The beauty of that counter occupies a central place in our house. We'd knocked down several walls to create an impressive space that always provoked compliments from visitors. The only thing separating living room from kitchen is that low, beautifully proportioned white counter that Jeff designed and I tiled. Sometimes, of course, the counter fills up with kitchen and family things—mail, juice glasses, Devin's toys and drawings. Now Marielle was giving it back its essence to make, at least, something right. ■

In 1990 our family made an important decision that in many ways softened the impact of Jeff's illness. We decided to begin home schooling the children. Jeff and I had always believed it the most effective and least invasive style of education and of life. We had read much of John Holt's writing and subscribed to home schooling newsletters such as *Growing without Schooling*. I had written for some of them.

Among the various other details of life, this interest in home schooling had not become a priority, especially since our neighborhood public school was a good one, by many standards, and our kids got along well there. Also, Jeff's illness had made us wary of introducing yet another demand on our time and energy, yet another way in which our household would differ from those of our kids' friends.

In 1985, however, I was sitting with two-week-old Devin on the bench around the goat statue in Rittenhouse Square when one of the other mothers came up to me. "Did I see your name in *Growing without Schooling?*" she asked me. It turned out that she was planning to do home schooling with her son, then two and a half. Over the next three years we kept in touch, and we finally formed a home schooling support group, meeting alternately at her house and mine. It was through her and that group that our family found the courage, the commitment, and the support to begin home schooling.

At first Bret, ten when he began home schooling, wanted

to use the same books and workbooks the school had lent us, and to follow the daily schedule his class had followed. However, this soon gave way to the unstructured home schooling I had envisioned. I began making up my own worksheets, Bret began directing his own learning (one of his favorite projects was combining our broken VCRs and TVs into a working color TV), and I began listing trips, family conversations, and some TV programs in the home schooling log that Pennsylvania law requires.

Bret, and soon Devin, thus learned (and learn) as they live and as they see us live—as they see us enjoy pursuing our own interests and passions. The amount of time spent on semiformal schoolwork has been far less than what I used to spend helping with homework (or, sometimes, smoothing out student-teacher relations). Certainly home schooling has not been difficult or inconvenient and did not, as I feared, pile stress upon dire straits.

Actually, home schooling made life less stressful. Our days were simpler, more flexible. The kids didn't have to go to bed early in order to be up for school the next day, and I used early mornings for writing. Bret had time to baby-sit or just play or be with Devin. (He also baby-sat for neighbors' families and earned some money, and this eased our financial worries.) And he was free to help with his dad. He was not forced to, but there were plenty of ages and stages when he wanted to, and he and Jeff often spent afternoons together fixing TVs and VCRs while I took Dev to the park or taught a workshop.

In general, the kids spent more time with us and over a greater spread of hours. This meant, among other things, that they saw what was going on and what we were going through, and they could better understand and relate to us. In fact Bret noticed how tired I was from lack of sleep and also saw, because of the family bed, why there was such lack of sleep, and he offered to take over some nights. (We paid him.)

I also believe that the kids were spared some school stress, which perhaps partly made up for the MS stress. Sometimes I wonder whether it was the very act of deciding to home school that made the difference. Having chosen and succeeded with a new life-style, our family felt empowered. Perhaps it was that empowerment that made up for some of our powerlessness surrounding the MS. ■

Still, the MS caused negative stuff between the kids and Jeff. Sometimes father and kids together were like a bunch of kids alone. Squabbling kids. One late evening, when Bret was going to be on with his dad, I was positively thirsty to get into that other room and sleep. I was three feet into the hallway when I heard "Mar!" I went back to hear what Jeff wanted to tell me and then found I couldn't relax. I went downstairs to unwind with writing and ice cream. But I was hearing increasing bickering between the two youngest, and soon Patty, on her way out from putting Jeff to bed, came into the kitchen and said, "Jeff's getting freaked out by the kids' fighting. You better go up there and see what you can do."

My therapist had taught me about setting limits. "I'm no better at it than anybody else," I told Patty. "If Jeff can't stop the fighting, then I can't either." And I didn't go up.

The fighting didn't stop. Fifteen minutes later, on my way into the other bedroom, I went in to collect Dev and take him to bed with me. He soon nursed himself to sleep, and me almost to sleep. But the screaming didn't stop. With only one kid in there, the fighting had to be Bret and Jeff. I could hear that it was mostly Jeff. "No! Put my leg *there!*" "Turn me *that* way." "No, *that* way." "Mar? Mar? I'm in pain. *Pain.*"

"So am I," I called back. I did not go in, and things did eventually quiet down.

"Well," I thought, "there are limits." I knew I had done the right thing. But still, a question nagged: Wasn't I perhaps just a mite influenced by my mother? My intellectual mother had once told me of a story she'd read whose hero was an artist of some kind. A sick person in the house called his name when he was in the throes of creation, and he didn't go; this time his art came first. There were stars in my mother's eyes. "No," I thought, "there are not stars in my eyes." And it wasn't creation I'd been in the throes of; it was fatigue. It wasn't a matter of my art but of my life. ∎

At the same time, there was humor in our lives. We created it, or we discovered it, especially at night in the family bed. Once Jeff was in bed and had used the first jar, we could all relax. "When is a jar not a jar?" Bret, then around ten, would call out.

Dev, four, would breathe or sigh or otherwise indicate that it was his turn to say something; then he'd shriek, "When it's a bedpan!"

"Right," Bret would go. "Now, when is a bedpan not a

bedpan?" Then, without waiting for an answer, "When it's turned the wrong way!"

We'd all shriek with delight. "And listen to this: Dad asks for a jar and halfway through we go, 'Oh, no! It's *not* a jar!' "

"Oh, no!" we'd exclaim in unison, and someone would ask, "What *is* it?"

Bret had the answer ready and waiting. "It's a door!"

That was pure nonsense, the kind of humor Jeff says he likes best, and his laugh was often the loudest of all.

"And if they discover a cure for MS"—this also from Bret—"and if Dad gets better, then he'll be the one to tuck Dev into bed and Mom'll be the one who'll talk on the phone all the time. Yeah," he continued, obviously pleased, perhaps defining something, "and Daddy'll go thrift shopping and Mommy'll do the solar energy."

"Yeah," I caught the ball, "and Mommy'll be the one to call 'Mar' and Dad'll hand Mom a jar or put Mom on the toilet or put Mom's right leg back and Mom's left leg forward."

We kept to that theme a while, laughing more and more loudly. Also, though, I was thinking: "You can bet Mom'll call 'Mar' a lot. At least at first."

Sometimes the fun felt extra positive and reassuring and smacked more of in-joking and of the culture of which we were unwilling members. I miss those days just a little. But I realize that, if Jeff were home now, we would probably have less and less of that kind of thing; it would have worn even more thin than it had begun to last year. Jeff would be needing thirty jars, not five or six, and there would be, besides the respirator, the feeding tube. When I read this page to Bret, he said, "We did have fun but not that often. Other families have fun more often."

The jokes without Jeff, jokes behind his back, jokes we shared with him later, were more sober. On occasion Jeff's parents would drive in from North Jersey, visit with us awhile, and then take Jeff plus attendant back with them for a few days. The kids and I felt free—suddenly, intensely, euphorically, and with very little guilt.

Wow! We could go out for ice cream! We could go to the park and stay until late afternoon! We could go to the movies! We could go up to Bret's room to play a video game without first excusing ourselves and assuring Jeff we'd hear him if he called.

The first night we all slept in the king-sized bed. Bret, eleven, lay down on Jeff's side and called to Devin, just four, "Jar!"

Devin brought over a pretend jar and the two started wrestling. "Turn me over!" yelled Bret, and they wrestled some more.

"No," I called from my side of the bed. "I need a jar again so you have to turn me back."

We were at it half an hour. "No, not the day jar, the night jar." "No, not that foot, the other foot." "Mar?" Pause. "Is the jar on right." "Mar, is the door closed?" Long pause. "But leave it open a little so the cat can go out."

"Oh, yeah," Bret kept interjecting, as we all were reminded of each separate thing. "Oh, yeah," we kept giggling.

After a while Bret said, "I guess if someone can't move, we might as well joke about it."

"Yes," I answered. "It's okay to."

We kept at it, trying to cover everything, trying to include every last one of Jeff's fears and foibles. We kept at it, reclaiming perspective, reclaiming sanity, reclaiming something, maybe reclaiming everything. And some of the time I thought, "It's partly the euphoria of having a good time with my kids and partly the kind of laughing when you're not happy." Also, sometimes Bret really did sound like Jeff, and it was a little scary. As though Jeff had somehow come back and I really did have to hand him a jar. Maybe we were all beating that fear to the punch.

Shortly after Jeff started to live at Inglis House we had a similar bantering. This time there was more to make fun of. "Can you check the jar? But don't touch the J-tube." "Is the waterbag flowing?" "Could you lower the blow tube?" And that new-fangled voice-activated device he eventually got rid of it; it didn't work, probably because he hasn't enough voice. Dev would mimic the robot voice. "TV. Phone. VCR." Then, "Jar, you idiot! What I want is a jar!"

"Sorry," I mimicked the machine. "I'm not programmed for jar." We were reclaiming again.

Often the fun would include our attendants. It would be especially unfair to Aurelio not to include the day of the triple play. Jeff was feeling nauseated due to a new health diet involving saltwater and what we called "raw refried beans." He was feeling pretty green; moreover, he had to toilet, and Aurelio, who was around at the time, put him on. A minute later Jeff announced that he had to lie down, so Aurelio took him off and laid him on the Oriental rug in the living room. A second after that Jeff began to throw up.

Then he began to defecate, and then he asked for a jar. I brought rags, and Aurelio placed them strategically, while Jeff kept screaming, "The rug! The rug!" In the midst of it all Aurelio quipped, "Triple play!" Jeff was the first to burst out laughing. ∎

Typical of the humor at well-spouse meetings are comments like these: "Oh, yes, my husband's bowel habits are regular. Every time the attendant's just left for the day, that's when he has to go." Or "That's all he ever says, all day long. 'Helen do this.' 'Helen do that.' I've finally figured out how to solve my problem. I'm going to change my name."

In phone conversations between meetings, my well spouse friend Fern and I often had a lot of laughs. One evening we had just settled down to talk and Jeff needed toilet. "Guess what," I said to Fern.

"I'll wait," she answered. Ten minutes later, just as we'd gotten reconnected, she said, "Marion, you want to hear something hysterical?"

"What?" I asked.

"*Jim* has to go on the toilet."

We burst out laughing. Ten minutes later, back once again on the phone together, "It's contagious!" we shrieked. "They timed it just right. They're in cahoots. They're all in cahoots. And I bet just now Barbara's and Peg's and Maggie's"—the other well spouses we knew—"I bet they all, just now, were put on the toilet—all at the same time."

Well spouses have a culture, a solidarity, that provides an opportunity for in-joking. But humor is not the answer to our problems. In fact, sometimes I am wary of humor. It can easily be misinterpreted. It can be used to deflect or mini-mize. Anyone reading about humor in my family might get the message that "it's not so bad." And it is so bad.

A sense of humor is not a sense of happiness. Laughing makes us happy only when we already are happy, and laughter without happiness can feel like a nightmare. Or like the laughter of losers.

Humor, sadness, fatigue, anger, love, stress—there were too many variables. In math, if a function is of three or more variables, you can't graph it, that is, you can't draw it, can't quite visualize it. With too many variables, you can't see what's going on. You write down equations, wave your hands about, and calculate. ■

a separate species: relationships
with the world and with ourselves

six

Well spouses often talk about how old friends
no longer come around. They add that they no
longer feel comfortable with old friends, and
they can't make new friends because they never go any-
where. "We don't fit in with married couples," they continue, "nor are we exactly swinging singles." Saying things
like this, some of them have tears in their eyes.

My own experience has been slightly different. While I
have contended with some of that isolation, I have also had
many good friends who have listened, if not understood.
Moreover, many of my friendships have been enhanced by
my being a well spouse; for example, a friend who just found
out that her forty-two-year-old husband might have Alzheimer's can turn to me for understanding. Some friendships have begun because of shared well-spouse experiences. A poet acquaintance became a friend when, at a
chance meeting at the local drugstore, she mentioned that a
lover of hers had died from complications of MS. A mother
in the park has a husband who's manic depressive, so we
always have long conversations.

However, one of my non-well-spouse friends recently confided that she has felt overawed by my circumstances. "Sometimes I find that I hesitate to share my own personal problems with you," she said. "I'm afraid they'll just pale in the light of yours." This friend did add, "You act in such a way that I usually don't feel that way."

Still, I join all well spouses in feeling some alienation from the world. Not only are we becoming a separate species from our ill spouses, we're becoming a separate species, period. Perhaps, to the rest of the world, *we're* the ones who are ill. The motto of the Well Spouse Foundation is, "When one is sick, two need help." In my book *The Level of Doorknobs* I talk about "the disabled family." Jeff's MS makes the entire household disabled.

I use the word *alienated* to describe how I've felt much of the time, although I have kept up many friendships, old and new . . . although I have been able to do nearly everything I've wanted to do, though maybe not as much of it as I've wanted . . . although being a well spouse has not kept me from writing, doing math, teaching, piano playing, singing, thrift shopping, and being a full-time, stay-at-home mother . . . although I've connected up with the world in the way I've wanted to . . . although I feel satisfied that I've been able to contribute what I have in me to contribute . . . and although it does not sound as though I've been isolated or alienated.

Our experience simply is not that of most people. A well spouse does not view things the way a non–well spouse does. "In social situations," says Fern, "or with relatives, other people are in their various normal stages, and they have various normal news, like ski trips and marriages and stuff. What can I talk about? I can say, 'Well, I had a whole hour to myself last week.' It feels like nothing, compared to what other people do. It's when I get together with other people that I realize how different I am. At home I don't quite realize, I take my life pretty much for granted." Recall that Fern is a working person, a professional; she also has a wide range of friends and goes on weekend trips, probably as often as anybody else. Still, she has the feeling of being different; there is always that threat, that tendency toward anger, bitterness, and alienation.

What I felt was confused. I couldn't believe that society, which included my friends and relatives, was allowing our dire straits to continue. As an adult, I understood that my attitude was at least slightly nonsensical or unrealistic; still, I felt betrayed. And when people (usually acquaintances rather than friends) said things like "We all have our crosses to bear" or "We have to be strong," I was either too furious to say much or too furious to keep my mouth shut. On the other hand, when people had the right attitude, when they sympathized, when they said anything approaching "You really have had a hard life" or "You got a bum rap" or "Yes, we all have our crosses to bear but you definitely got more than your share," I sometimes got furious, too. Their words rubbed my situation in, made it all extra true, even felt mocking or sadistic. I heard behind their words, "Yes, we do know. We do know what you're going through. And we're letting it happen, anyway." At the very least I felt disappointed.

Now I think I know the answer to the question Why

don't they rescue us? For the same reason we don't rescue our ill spouses.

Still, those two months I was down with a broken ankle, Jeff's brother could have come on a regular basis instead of just dropping in every once in a while, often when an attendant was there anyway. And Louise's husband could have said, "I'll be over to put him to bed every Tuesday and Thursday evening," instead of us having to call him all the time. My friends who were mothers could have said, "Tell Devin he can count on Jeremy and me coming by and taking him to the park every Monday." It would have taken some of the worry out of our lives if they had offered something regular, something we could count on more than once. We could have used an organized support system; I would have loved it if our friends had all gotten together and worked out some giant plan.

During that broken-ankle era only Aurelio came several times a week. In fact, overhearing me tantrum one evening, he boomed the welcome words, "Okay, I'm moving back in for awhile." Only Aurelio seemed to understand that in times of dire straits, everyone is responsible. During that broken-ankle period, it was only Aurelio from whom we didn't feel alienated.

Again, many people seemed to think our dire straits were just plain stress. "You can do it," they'd say. "You just *feel* like you can't." "It's beyond all that," is what well spouses say about those kinds of encounters. "It's just a whole different realm."

People who'd say, "I'm worried about you, Marion," or "I have a feeling you're not saying how bad things really are" were often those to whom I truly was not saying how bad things really were because they were not the people I confided in or who would listen if I did confide in them. Still, it felt like criticism. Or like that case worker who grabbed me to her, demanding I cry on her shoulder. It didn't feel like harsh criticism, just criticism. Or advice. But definitely not praise or acknowledgment. To any variant of "You're not saying how bad things really are," I'd sometimes quip, at least in my mind, "Oh, are you curious to know how bad things really are? Then buy my poetry books!"

But the hurt went deep. And suppose, I'd speculate, someone said, "Marion talks too much about how bad things are." Was anyone saying that? What did I want them to say? I wanted them to say "She's expressing it exactly enough, just right, exactly how and how much she should, neither too little nor too much."

As always among friends, sometimes mine seemed to understand and then suddenly didn't. Sandy and I got together for dinner one evening after she'd just landed a great job that involved taking people out to expensive restaurants about twice a week on "the account." Three gorgeous, sensitive, passionate men had answered her ad in the *Philadelphia Magazine* personals, and none seemed to mind that she'd stipulated no sex because of fear of AIDS. "They're happy to just kiss," she told me. So I started telling her that if I were to decide to seek other men besides Jeff, or if (meaning when) Jeff died, I'd put an ad in the personals that would read something like: "My experiences include getting a Ph.D. in math, publishing nine poetry books, losing a full-term baby, gaining four full-term babies, and having a husband with MS. I'm very, very vulnerable but strong in ways you can't imagine." "And," I told Sandy, "I wouldn't just say no sex; I'd say no kissing."

"Oh," said Sandy, "you might surprise yourself."

Many well spouses have surprised themselves, and many haven't. Many, indeed, have been disappointed. Well spouses have a range of different feelings and needs concerning sex, or companionship, with people other than their ill spouses. Many are too tired, too taken up, too a lot of things, to be interested in sex or even companionship. The issue of extramarital affairs is not simple to a well spouse, and Sandy's comment felt presumptuous. It disturbed, upset, and alienated me. I was in no mood to be surprised, even by myself, and I felt very, very vulnerable.

I felt subtly alienated even from people who were helping us. During two of those broken-ankle weeks Verna from Blue Cross came in five hours a day. She cooked, cleaned, took Dev to the park, did anything I'd ask, and cheerfully. She was attentive, intelligent, and compassionate. But to me, compassion felt strangely nightmarish. It smacked of hospitals, blood, and nurses with strange ways. Maybe that's part of the definition of compassion, that it must come from strangers.

Doris, too, the tough, cheerful nurse who tended daily to Jeff's bedsore, was smart, entertaining, and compassionate. But she was still nurse. Still hospital. And full of instructions, though slightly apologetic, as to what I'd be responsible for once her two weeks were up.

Well, I thought, what can anybody do? Compassionate can't be the same thing as tender. Tender comes with knowing, with loving, with time. And right there, right then, all that was tender—meaning my husband and my children—was powerless. ∎

The whole situation was alienating. In some sense, I was even alienated from my own home. I often didn't understand things. Big math Ph.D., I didn't know how to load the family camera or use the computer in Elle's room. And it was a while before I learned how to operate the VCR. I had neither the time nor the energy nor the interest. I had no room in my life for more skills, especially unpaid skills.

One midnight the doorbell rang, and I went to peek through the hole. It was no one I recognized. "Yes?" I called.

"It's the security guard," said the voice. "I'd like to talk to you."

I realized he was some stranger wanting money. I didn't know whether he planned to ask for it or just get it, but I had not opened, not come remotely close to opening, the door. Nevertheless for one small minute, my feeling was, "Oh, the security guard. Sure. Naturally. Come on in." For certainly, I thought, neighbors must have noticed how strange and suspicious our house and family were. The trike lift, the trikes themselves, Jeff never out, Aurelio always around, not to mention all the characters. "It's no surprise they're investigating," I thought. "It's no wonder they sent the security guard."

Sometimes I felt alienated from the community. On late dark nights, being out in the streets felt strange. One midnight, coming home from a well-spouse meeting, I found myself peeking ahead, and behind, buildings, porches, alleys. Patrolling, like our cat. Not believing that God or police or anything else would protect me. Believing, perhaps, that they would protect everyone *except* me. At the meeting a seventy-year-old woman had told us about "baby-duty" (that is, toilet); another seventy-year-old woman had talked about getting robbed by attendants; I had once again described nights and toilet. I'd gotten the feeling that no one is looking out for anyone.

The night that the police had come to our door and asked, "Were you screaming? Are you all right?" Suppose I had answered, "No, I'm not all right. I'm being raped and molested"? And then suppose I'd gone into detail about nights, lifting, and toilet? Would they have said, "Oh, we don't mean that kind of rape. We don't protect anyone from that kind of rape." (Just like Volunteers of America didn't have "that kind of volunteers.")

Walking along that street, I thought, "It's only a matter of time before I get raped. Not molested, but raped. And not that kind of rape, but actual rape. And then if one of the attendants actually did rape me, Jeff would somehow convince himself that it didn't happen, or that it was okay. Maybe I'd be convinced, too. After all, a good attendant is hard to find."

The rules are different, or feel different, when you're a well spouse. We're second- or third-class citizens, so naturally we feel alienated from the community. And we also feel alienated from all the smaller communities to which we belong based on our individual interests, beliefs, and circumstances. Our age group, for example, or our religious or choral group; the black community, gay community, home-schooling community. Being well spouses does not prevent but does complicate our memberships in our various niches.

Kathy's husband was totally paralyzed in a sports accident; her boys at the time were ages three and six. At the annual well-spouse convention she stood up and told us all, "When I was at my son's school play last week, I felt very alienated; I just was not like the other mothers." And my friend and neighbor Joy, whose husband is manic depressive, says, "When I talk with the other mothers at the park, I just can't relate; they talk about their problems like 'Jimmy won't take a nap' and 'Johnny won't eat his spinach' and to me those just don't seem like problems." Well-spouse mothers feel alienated from the community of mothers.

"In the work itself, everything's fine," says Fern of her job as a family therapist. "In fact, it's a real escape from my life at home, and it seems easy, compared to what I have to do at home. And if any of my clients have a situation where they're dealing with chronic illness, then—unless the situation is too similar to mine—my own experience helps. But at staff meetings, when everyone socializes a little beforehand, some people talk about personal stuff like 'My child was up at 2:00 A.M. last night.' Well, I can't say, 'My husband was up at 2:00, and at 3:00, and at 4:00, and I had to clean him up.' I can't say things like that. It would be too shocking, too distracting. It would take up too much time. So I'm alienated sometimes at work; I'm not normal."

As a feminist, I had always been careful not to play into the "woman as long sufferer" role. But I was suffering, and I was suffering long. I was not refusing to do nights, lifting, and toilet, and I was answering each and every "Mar!" I did understand that true feminism means being woman identified and doesn't preclude being a well spouse. But still, at times, I worried that my feminism might be at stake.

Jeff's illness naturally led to our family's involvement in the disability community, but that community does not always feel like my community. The disability movement is not the well-spouse movement. Disability advocates take into account the cause of care givers, but that's not their emphasis. Many well spouses have said, for example—and I can see the pain and hurt in their faces—that what solves the problem of sex and sexuality for disabled people is often quite inadequate for the partners of disabled people.

Also, my well-spouse poems are not always chosen for disability anthologies; often editors have said they want to stick with writers who are themselves disabled. "I *am* disabled," I have told them. "Anyone who does nights, lifting, and toilet is very definitely physically challenged." I understand that I am probably wrong, that my disability is not quite the same. But I have often felt disabled—and alienated from anyone who claimed I wasn't. ■

On one of my broken-ankle mornings four and a half years ago we received a phone call around 7:30 A.M. from our regular attendant. He wasn't going to be able to make it today; his ten-month-old son was in the hospital with a high fever. We were desperate. Jeff had to be at work by 1:00, to teach his first class of the semester. I hit the Resources for Living Independently list, which gives names of four attendants at a time. The first guy I rang up asked what

salary the service pays. I told him, and he screamed at me, "You're a real con artist. You're pocketing the money. I've been in this business a long time." I'm sure he would have gone on and on in this vein had I not hung up on him.

"How dare he talk to me like that?" I screamed to Jeff, shaking and sobbing. Although I soon calmed down, the experience brought home once again the awareness that I'd been forced to compromise. I never liked hiring house-keepers or taking taxis. I worried about being exploitative. And now I was forced to hire attendants, to appear horribly rich to nonwhite, non-middle-class people, none of whom would know that we'd bought this huge center-city house with settlement money from a case involving the death of our two-day-old daughter. I felt bourgeois and politically incorrect—I'd worked through the guilt, but this just wasn't my way.

Well spouses often feel weak, ineffective, and perhaps ashamed and guilt ridden. Our belief systems are often threatened. We're forced, or feel we're forced, to go against our beliefs, our habits, our life-styles, and our expectations. We can't or mayn't be good mothers, or good grandmothers, or good feminists, or good disability advocates; we can't keep in touch with certain friends, keep up with cultural events, or attend church or shul as often as we'd like or feel we should. We can't take jobs because we have to stay home and be care givers, or we *must* take jobs because we've lost our ill spouse's income.

We always believed we'd be "better" care givers when the time came. Or we were modest; we believed we'd never touch dress or undress our mates in front of others (meaning attendants). Like Arin as a young teenager, we believed the government would come to our aid; we believed in government and in health-care systems. We believed in our relatives and friends, that when the time came they would be there for us. We believed love conquers all.

I used to say, "People don't want solutions, only problems," and I prided myself on seeking and usually finding solutions to many of my problems, especially with respect to being a mother. Now I was stuck with a problem whose partial solutions, which I worked very hard to find, made little dent.

"If I didn't have this situation," says Fern, "I would be different." Indeed, how much of our selves has been taken from us? How much have our relationships with our very selves been undermined?

Friends would remark how tired I looked. If I was getting up twenty times a night, I must look tired. "But I *don't* look tired," I'd think. "In fact, just this morning that woman on the subway, who doesn't know I get up twenty times a night, was telling me how pretty I look—'alert,' she said, 'alive.'" I don't even feel tired, at least not today. Others can't help being swayed by their knowledge of our situation, and we can't help being swayed by what others say and think. Is there a typical care-giver image out there—a prejudice, a stereotype? And does it alienate us from ourselves?

Our houses are messy, or messier than they would be. I'd find whole pieces of shit in the laundry, because attendants can't or don't do toilet and washing at the same time. Our bodies, ourselves—our houses, ourselves. The people we associate with so much of the time are more downtrodden than they would be. Other ill people besides our spouses, other well spouses, attendants, especially the characters. Our lives in general are less in control than they would be.

So many variables can make for confusion. Where do our selves end and our situations begin? What is the connection between us and what is done to us? If you're so smart, why ain't you rich? applies to us less than If we're so smart, why are we barely even poor? If we're so well adjusted, if we've been through therapy and support groups, why aren't we in control of our lives?

Maybe we have a handle on it. Maybe, like Fern, and like me, we continually take stock and are able to keep up with this stock taking. Still, I have felt many times like a sucker, an enabler, a professional victim. How could anyone allow any man to do these things to her? No one, no molester, makes anyone do *toilet*. No wonder we feel weak.

On the other hand, society also calls us strong. Because we do nights, lifting, and toilet, we're viewed as strong, and sometimes it's assumed we're strong in all ways. For example, do we only imagine that people who know we're well spouses don't open doors for us? If we have time to shop and may leave our homes, do we dress in practical clothes, where otherwise we might not? Do I like to create a "feminine" look with my long dresses and long hair to counteract that image? Is one of the reasons I kept having babies so I could be, if a "strong" woman, at least a woman?

Does strong sometimes translate into bossy or insensitive? Have we actually become bossy and insensitive? Do we wonder whether we've become that way? Do we bend over backwards not to be that way? If a care giver stereotype exists, is it ever self-perpetuating?

The question What does everybody think of us? was, for me, never entirely answered, but well spouses generally agree that people don't think about us much at all. "All the attention is on my spouse. Out in the streets, everyone notices the person in the wheelchair, never the person pushing the wheelchair." That lament has been voiced countless times at well-spouse support-group meetings. In *Mainstay*, Maggie Strong calls it the "invisibility" of the well spouse.

I fought hard against invisibility. If anyone dared say, "It's so hard for him," I'd snap, "And it's also hard for me and the kids."

Eight years ago a neighbor asked, "Hi, Mar, how's Jeff?"

"Fine," I answered. "His wife just had a baby."

I related that incident in *The Level of Doorknobs*, and Maggie Strong later mentioned it in several of her presentations, in the well-spouse newsletter, and, so I heard one day from several friends and relatives, on Oprah Winfrey. That story has also gotten back to me at various well-spouse gatherings. Well spouses seem bolstered by hearing that kind of retort.

But I was not always so plucky. One Sunday—attendant's day off—Jeff had been calling "Mar!" with more than his usual frequency. All the phone calls had been for him (friends, physics colleagues, solar-energy contacts), and I had to help with most of them. At the end of the day I had finally had the opportunity to take a shower, because Jeff was in the midst of a long phone call, writing a physics paper with someone I'll call Stu. So I knew I wouldn't need to help him with another phone call and that he wouldn't need to call for me; his nose, for example, never itched while he was on the phone.

So I was in the shower, and just as I was beginning to truly rejuvenate Bret called up to me from downstairs. "Mom? The phone! It's for you."

Ah, finally! A call for me! Friend? I wondered. Student? Publisher? Although I wasn't quite dried off, I grabbed for that phone. (We had a phone in every room, including the bathrooms, to accommodate Jeff.)

"Marion? Hi!" said the voice. "This is Stu." The physicist Jeff had just been talking to. "Jeff told me to call back and ask for you. He was having trouble holding on to the receiver and he asked me to call back and ask for you because . . . well, he knew he wouldn't be able to answer and hold the receiver so . . . "

My heart sank. My temper rose. I wished I could be inaudible as well as invisible. "Huh?" I said. "I'm in the shower; you'll have to wait." But no matter how long he waited, no matter how long *I* waited, I wouldn't be in the mood to help Jeff with that call from Stu. I had to do it without being in the mood. And I had to be (or had to feel as though I was) an accessory to the invisibility plot.

I had this same feeling whenever I walked down the street alone and I happened to pass another "disabled family." Especially if it was the husband in the trike and the wife and kids walking alongside him, I longed to say something; I longed to make some contact. But I never did because, in order to make that contact, I needed Jeff and the trike and the kids with me. In those cases I felt invisible in the opposite way from the example with Stu; it was my care-giver identity I was being deprived of. I felt split. Indeed, when I wasn't with Jeff, I had what the disability movement calls "an invisible disability." And why, I wondered, didn't a disabled family ever pass by when Jeff and the kids were with me? Probably, I see now, because increasingly Jeff wasn't with me in the streets.

Less than a year ago, I felt strangely bitter over an incident that deprived me of my care-giver identity in another way. A bunch of us were playing *Therapy,* a kind of trivia game. I got the card that read: "Mary wakes up gradually. Sally wakes up suddenly. Who remembers her dreams better, Mary or Sally?"

"Aha!" I thought. "I wake up suddenly, or am awakened suddenly. And that dream life just slips away. I don't remember my dreams. But those few times when I wake up by myself, not by jar, I wake up gradually and I have time to note each detail of my dream as I say good-bye to it, and I remember my dream well."

So I answered, "Mary. The one who wakes up gradually."

But the card was turned over, and it was Sally, the sudden awakener.

I felt betrayed, shortchanged. Insult had been added to injury. My experience and expertise at waking up suddenly had not paid off. Even when being a well spouse connects up with the world, it connects up wrong. Indeed, my life, and therefore my self, had not helped me; my well-spouse self had not helped me.

I was in a funny position, was how I often thought of it. The role it puts you in, is how my friend Nancy thought of it. It was a hard-to-peg role. To my husband I was wife, mother, master, servant, warden, prisoner, boss, secretary, know-it-all, captor, captive; I was mousy, strong, weak, and so on. They were roles I fought all the way. ■

preparing for his ghost: about loss

seven

About five years ago Sophie, a new friend who is an artist a generation older than I, had me over for lunch. Her apartment was beautiful, enhanced by and integrated with her sculpture. It came out that she had been a well spouse for thirty years. "First it was heart attack," she told me, "and it was at a time when doctors were advising him to take it easy—"

"Which meant," I interjected, "you taking it hard." She nodded.

"Then it was Parkinson's," she continued. "And next . . . well, I now believe it was Alzheimer's."

We talked awhile about the nuts and bolts of it and then she said, "I was a mean care giver. I did everything, but I didn't do it lovingly." Especially at the end, she added. Her children, other relatives, and friends had offered neither understanding nor support; they'd expected her to do it all, cheerfully, unquestioningly, to live up to those marriage vows with no help, to conform to that world image of woman as eternal care giver.

"I feel horribly guilty," she said. "You know, you don't remember how hard it is, you don't remember the bad things; what you remember is how bitchy you were, and you think 'Now, what was I so bitchy about?' "

"You won't feel that way," she said. "You're working things through. You have the support of your family, and you're in touch with your feelings. You won't have that problem."

I hoped she was right. I think she was right. But I'm careful about a lot of things. Careful to keep the support of my family, to keep in touch with my feelings, to keep not being a "mean care giver," and mainly to keep remembering what it was like, how "bad" it was, which means, in part, to keep writing about it. Writing—my journal, my poems, this book—has been an act of necessity, maybe an act of desperation. I want to make sure I won't forget "what I was so bitchy about" and I won't feel "horribly guilty" like Sophie.

I call it "preparing for his ghost." I have been through the process before. The first ghost I prepared for was my mother's, beginning eighteen years ago after my father died suddenly in the night, heart attack; I was thirty-three at the time; Elle and Arin were six and three. My father and I had not been particularly close—in fact, there were tensions, mostly because my father was so repressed he was not particularly close to anyone. Family relations had been such that I was consumed, and later haunted, less by grief than by the impact of what I called "the power of the family." My father had given his body to science; there was no funeral. My parents had been atheists, so there was no sitting shiva. There was, however, plenty of congregating at that house—too many, too concentrated, too close for comfort. The tensions were aggravated. I had my own inner tensions; guilt issues especially came to the forefront.

I wrote poems about it, and perhaps the most helpful was a two-liner that came to me suddenly: "I am preparing / for my mother's ghost." I meant that I was going to make sure that, when my mother died, I wouldn't be consumed in this way. In particular, I wanted to make sure that I wouldn't be consumed with questions of guilt or other unfinished business.

In conscious preparation for her ghost I wrote more poems, longer poems, in which I worked through a lot of the tension, and sources of tension, between my mother and me. I shared my poems with her even more than I already had, and I wrote her a letter about all the issues we hadn't shared. She wrote me back, a short letter saying essentially that she loved me but wasn't strong enough emotionally to deal with those things. So I dealt alone; preparing for her ghost was a one-sided effort. A few years later, when she died from a massive stroke over a period of sixteen days, I found that the preparations had been sufficient. Preparing for her ghost had paid off. In particular, her ghost did not interfere with my happiness when Bret was born seven weeks later. And five years afterward, in therapy, that letter and my mother's answer helped me deal with her by then older ghost. ■

For the past sixteen and a half years, I have been preparing for my husband's ghost. The issues are different and there are fewer of them; Jeff and I communicate and so have avoided the kind of tension that existed in the family I was born into. Still, I think of Sophie. And I worry and feel afraid.

Have I been a "mean care giver"? Jeff didn't like the tantrums, but they weren't mean, only desperate. And I never hit him or anybody else, and I never threw things or broke things or lost my senses. No, I assure myself, I wasn't mean.

Have I been "doing it lovingly" enough? Often I have. In the midst of a transfer we'd sometimes hug. And toilet, at least at the beginning, had intimate overtones. Now I sit with Jeff lovingly, my hand around his, his around mine. (I have to put his around mine. Just a few days ago, I remarked, "I know that was just a spasm, but it still feels good, your gripping my hand," and he smiled.) I sit with him, sometimes lie with him, if he's been placed sufficiently to one side of the bed so there's room for me. Long quiet looks, maybe some kissing, even petting, as much as the feeding tube and the catheter will allow. And I felt loving, at least some of the time. When I didn't feel loving, I acknowledged that. I never pretended—certainly not to myself—that I felt loving when I didn't. Jeff's mother once wrote me, "Thank you for being such a loving wife to Jeff." Did she use the word *loving* casually, or had she chosen it specifically?

Was I loving enough so I won't, later, feel "horribly guilty"? I recall my mother saying, of my sister's and my childhood, "I was very loving, but when I think about it now, it seems I wasn't loving enough." Is it ever loving enough? I've been rearing my last child based on the philosophy in *The Continuum Concept,* which means I've been with Devin almost constantly. I breastfed on demand for many years, and I breastfed lovingly. No question that not only was I loving enough but I felt, and feel, loving enough. Over the years, will I forget that? About Devin and about Jeff? It all feels too slippery. If it's not now, it's not enough.

Loving, Sophie, cannot save us. No matter how much loving, we forget it; no matter how little bitching, we remember it. With or without loving there is guilt. Maybe "horrible guilt." And regret. And frustration. Time does funny things. Time used lovingly is still time. And it's still used. It still, that is, passes. It's all far too slippery.

And I don't know, Sophie, to what extent working things through, expressing my feelings, and having the support of my family and friends will help me to meet Jeff's ghost. I won't know for sure until it happens. Now that I am freed from nights, lifting, and toilet, I do feel more loving, less mean; I have more perspective, and better perspective. More strongly, and more often, I feel confident that I am prepared, or almost prepared, for his ghost, and that I will not be consumed with "horrible guilt."

Recently I told Bret about Sophie; he had asked me, Why write about nights, lifting, and toilet? Why remember it? Why talk about it? "Well," I said, "one of the reasons is so I don't wind up feeling horribly guilty like Sophie—in particular, about the tantrums. And," I added, "so I won't ever change my mind and let Dad come back home."

And so, if they send him back, I run away.

And so I won't ever advise any other well spouse to change her mind and let her nursing-home spouse come home.

For me, part of preparing for this ghost is to keep him a ghost.

For I realize that Jeff is a ghost now. He's sick, with no

movement whatever below the neck, and he's away; maybe he's half a ghost. I understand that I've been thinking of my escape as happening in two stages: First, he goes into a nursing home; Second, he dies. Another thing I realize is that I'm doing well with that half ghost. Half escaping has not rendered me consumed with issues.

Still, preparing for a ghost is hard. It can be a task. It's certainly a process. We work at it, through many questions, much brainstorming. People who lose a loved one unexpectedly and suddenly often wish they had been given time to prepare. I know that's a mixed blessing.

We try to get in touch with what's happening to us, but we're so used to it, it's almost impossible to feel the impact. We try to get that deathbed feeling. Or we try to get in touch with the highest form of our love, the best memories. Or we try to build new memories. We try to give our ill spouses the best possible farewell.

But in order to give them any farewell at all, we need to feel that farewell. We need to feel sad. Sadness about something that has not yet happened or that has been happening for years is difficult to sustain. ■

Well-spouse grieving differs from other grieving, and from both society's and our own expectations. Like our spouses' illnesses, the grief is chronic. Long—as long as life—and complete with exacerbations and remissions. Even the exacerbations can feel chronic, that is, not acute.

Sixteen years ago, when we first heard the diagnosis, I did not cry. I did not even feel sad. For one thing, I was seven months pregnant. For another, Jeff was walking and weight lifting. The worst hadn't happened yet. The diagnosis was about the distant future. It was hard, even impossible, to feel sad, angry, or anything except denial, perhaps even a rather willing acceptance. It's probably as easy to accept a verdict of death in twenty or so years as a verdict of death in fifty or so years, which is what all of us have to accept. It reminds me of the joke where someone says, "I read in the paper today that the world's going to end in a trillion years." Someone else answers, "Whew! For a minute there I thought you said a million."

Well-spouse loss and grief is gradual. And gentle. To be completely honest, it's a piece of cake compared to nights, lifting, and toilet. It's also a piece of cake compared to the acute grief I felt when our baby Kerin died. That was pure grief; there were no issues involved, no guilt. I had not needed to prepare for her ghost. Next to that grief, the loss of my parents pales. And so does the very gradual, chronic loss through which I am going now. Through much of it, I have in fact been happy. I have certainly not been kept from happiness over other things—the kids, writing, life itself, various happinesses with Jeff. Chronic grief has not interfered with the process of living.

I once made another distinction between my griefs over Jeff and over the baby, Kerin. The loss of Kerin implied, I realized almost immediately, a new live baby, or the thought of one. I was preparing, not for a ghost, but for a new live person. (I was also preparing for the possibility of another ghost, that is, another dead baby.) My journal from that period is entitled "An Ambitious Sort of Grief." It was good, and hopeful, to have ambition along with sadness, but it was also difficult. Grieving and anticipating at the same time made me feel disoriented. Still, an ambitious sort of grief had obvious advantages. One of them was Bret. Another (maybe the same) was hope.

At one time I thought this grief over Jeff was the very opposite of ambitious. Yet I have discovered that on some vague level I expect to be compensated for it in some big way. I fantasize, for example, that maybe, because of the MS, Jeff's solar collector invention makes it; he connects up with some disability advocate who happens to have money and be interested in solar. Or else my writing makes it; one of my well-spouse books becomes a best-seller. Or maybe Jeff or I or both of us discover a cure and make it big in that way. Something special, something grandiose.

Fern tells me that she feels ambitious in a way similar to my ambitious feelings after losing the baby. "I'm excited about the future," she says. "Things I'll be able to do after he dies—maybe a new marriage." She pauses and ponders. "I'm also a little afraid. I'm afraid I won't do any of it."

"But that's part of ambition," I suggest. "Ambition includes fear. If it were certainty, it wouldn't be called ambition."

And so, for a while, Fern and I discuss our ambitious griefs. And I realize anew that all griefs are ambitious. ∎

If I had my choice of griefs, I'd probably choose chronic. However, chronic grief can feel scary. Detached. Unreal. It seems weird to be in the midst of a tragedy and to not quite feel it.

"It's such a tragedy," said a friend.

"I don't feel it that way," I answered.

To be so used to it that you can't feel, or can't often feel, makes the impact surreal. Not to be saying farewell to your true love in a final tragic deathbed scene feels strange.

"Jeff dead. Jeff gone." It is difficult to write those words, but I don't cry or tremble. I am too used to the idea. Moreover, I am not totally averse to it; a large part of me has wanted it to be fact. Nights, lifting, and toilet weren't that long ago. And on many days when I visit Jeff, he greets me in an especially weak voice, with an especially long list of complaints about how the nurse's aides are late getting him out of bed or answering the call bell . . . days when he asks me to wipe his nose . . . days when the mail brings a larger-than-life medical bill that I'm not certain Blue Cross will pay.

Chronic grief feels strange. Especially to someone who has experienced acute grief, and many well spouses, being people, have. (Three other members of my well-spouse group have lost a child.) Lately I have had several dreams about the eventuality. In one of them, in a deathbed scene, I go to Jeff, stay with him, and whisper, "Oh. Oh. I love you. Don't die. Please don't die." I keep whispering that again and again until I wake up. The dream felt like a play about Jeff dying. I was pretending to be saying "I love you. Please don't die." Or maybe I was pretending and truly saying it at the same time. Chronic grief can be confusing, slippery. It's hard to get a grip on, to keep in touch with. It can feel like denial, even when it isn't. Or it can sometimes feel like no grief at all.

I realize that, gradually, Jeff is no longer the largest part of my life. With chronic grief you separate; you unbond. And so chronic grief can make you feel guilty for not grieving acutely, not hurting so much. Your husband is dying, and you're not crying. What's the matter with you, or with your marriage? Especially if other strong issues in the marriage exist independent, or seemingly independent, of the disease, other reasons besides nights, lifting, toilet, and finances for you to want to be rid of your ill spouse. Especially, that is, if you already feel guilty.

One night around the time the movies *Ghost* and *Truly Madly Deeply* were showing, I dreamt that I was watching a play about a young couple. The woman in my dream was dead. Invisible, inaudible, bodiless. At night she came to her lover's room, just to be with him. Sometimes he felt her presence, sometimes he didn't. One night she wasn't invisible or inaudible. He uttered a cry of joy, and they began making love. Then he freaked out. "I'm making love with a dead woman," he thought. He ran from the room, then from the house.

Outside, friends, neighbors, family, maybe some of the characters in *Ghost* were congregating in his front yard, and they tried to convince him to go back inside. "You're missing out," they told him. "One night, only one night, and soon she'll be gone. And you're not seizing the moment."

I woke up asking, "Just like I'm not seizing Jeff? Should I be seizing Jeff?" Then I woke up further. "But it's not a *moment*." ("That's right," said Fern when I told her that dream. "It's not a moment.")

That was the right answer, but I tormented myself anyway. "I don't feel like seizing the moment. And it's not for just one night, or one day; it's five, ten years. And he's not here suddenly, nor will he be gone suddenly. He's here chronically, going chronically. Maybe I wish it could be sudden, maybe I wish I could seize the moment, but with chronic illness it's not like that; it's just not. Dammit, people outside, it's not."

I have written here about how being a well spouse alienates one from the community. In that dream the man was literally alienated from the community, from the neighborhood. And chronic grief also alienates us from the bereavement community. We are not bereaved in quite the same way as many people in bereavement groups. As Fern says, "We can't even go to bereavement groups." Our grieving seems to violate various rules and might upset the members of the group who are grieving acutely.

Perhaps another dream I had in those days will help clarify the plight of the chronic griever. In that dream it wasn't Jeff dying but our oldest son, Arin, who was killed in an automobile accident. Everyone was at a long table, passing around the urn with Arin's ashes in it and making speeches. When it came my turn I protested, "I'm not ready yet."

They insisted. So I began, slowly, matter-of-factly, and bitterly. "Every day lately," I said, "something horrible happens, and I see this day is no exception." The people all murmured "Uh-huh" like some of the professionals in real life whenever I mentioned nights, lifting, and toilet. I continued anyway. "So I'm not feeling anything just yet. I have to wait until I realize that this something is more horrible than the usual somethings."

I woke up superimposing the dream upon the day of Jeff's death. I probably won't believe it for a while. The funeral and other arrangements will just feel like regular things, horrible or annoying things, just more things I have to do concerning him.

Maybe I'll even think, "So what else is new?"

Dammit, people outside, so what else is new? ∎

where do we stand?
the second conspiracy of silence
eight

Where do we stand? It took me years to voice this question in this way. Meanwhile I asked other questions. Vague, silly-sounding, perhaps child-ish and self-centered, groping questions. Suppose I was so tired from lack of sleep that I couldn't think clearly? Or couldn't think at all? Suppose I was like two women in a long-ago dream, encased in glass, seen but not heard, not felt, not even sensed? Then would it be meaningless or ridiculous for friends, relatives, social workers, and some-times even other well spouses to say, "You have to help yourself"?

Suppose it's impossible for us to help ourselves? Suppose not only our bodies but also our minds are encased in glass, or concrete? Suppose we don't *have* our minds; sup-pose we're tired or asleep or drugged or dead? Then, God, *then* would you help us, even though we're not helping ourselves?

We had, of course, despite being that tired, already helped ourselves, and we'd helped ourselves to whatever help was available from the community, from relatives, from friends;

I'd written a book on asking for help. And I was still doing nights, lifting, and toilet, and answering to "Mar!"

How dire did our straits have to be? And in order for what to happen?

Maybe people just didn't know? Even though I talked about it, even though I'd called a family meeting, even though I was far from in the closet about it at parties and on the park bench, maybe people still didn't know. After all, hadn't Freda, my best friend who lives in Staten Island, two hours away by car, told me that, until she'd come to spend a weekend in our house, she hadn't really known what my life was like?

How much did people have to know? How dire did our straits have to be? Did we have the right to compare our situation to a concentration camp? After all, the holocaust didn't last a lifetime. What about a prison? After all, prisoners are allowed to sleep at night. Is "hard labor" harder than lifting and toilet?

Sometimes, instead of "dire straits," I'd use the word *just-terrible,* the undefinable *just-terrible* from my childhood, the word I reserved for prisons, capital punishment, and children's parents dying, especially if it was because they couldn't afford doctors. Yet why was this just-terrible different from the others? Perhaps because it was in my hands, or apparently in my hands. Or perhaps it seemed more just-terrible simply because it was here and now.

I only recently found a dictionary word for just-terrible. That word is *untenable,* and it felt important to know there was a word for it, and that others had made it up.

Still, how untenable were my straits? When something is untenable, do you have the right to call for help? To try to escape? Where do you stand?

I wondered if I had the right to be rescued. When my husband was in the hospital, I'd watch it take five nurses to do what I always did at home by myself. Sometimes I, or Jeff, would let the five nurses know that. Usually they'd go "Uh-huh," or truly not hear us, but every once in a while they'd exclaim, "You mean you do this all by yourself?"

My hopes would rise. "Gee," I'd think, "maybe they'll realize how just-terrible my situation is and rescue me. Talk to the main social worker or something." When that didn't happen I'd think, "Maybe I just haven't said enough." Maybe there had to be *six* nurses doing what I usually did alone.

One particularly caring nurse took me aside. "Your situation is pretty unusual," she said. "Are you okay?"

"Not really," I answered. "I am ready for some change, and I would like it if you'd see about it, and tell me about any resources I don't yet know about."

But nothing ever happened from that, or from any of the other nurses and social workers to whom I hinted or articulated my feelings. Didn't "unusual" mean "dire"? ∎

Bret burned out. Beverly burned out. Arin had burned out years ago. "How come I can't burn out?" I wondered. "Or can I?"

If someone leaves a baby on your doorstep, you don't have to take it. You can—in fact, you must—call the police or an orphanage or an adoption agency. But neither the police nor orphanages nor adoption agencies do toilet. Perhaps there were no "resources," no "programs," for me.

If we were stranded on a desert island, could a plane come, look us over, then decide not to rescue us? Could they say the insurance, or the grant, doesn't cover it? Could they begin to rescue us and then, literally, drop us midway?

Nuts-and-bolts questions arose out of specific circumstances every day. Should we call 911? Should we call sick-assist? Should we report talking-to-himself William to the service? Should we fire Patty? Did we have the right to take any of these actions? Each strait had to be evaluated separately, for adequate direness.

Those questions concerned our rights as citizens. Were we citizens? Even second-class citizens? To what class of society did we belong? To me our home smacked of ghetto, what with the smells, the sounds, and some of the characters. By association, if nothing else, our standard of living had gone down considerably. I also felt, sometimes, self-conscious complaining about the dire straits in front of the attendants, because I suspected that some of them came from backgrounds that would make my complaining sound bourgois. I wondered what they thought of me, and especially if they thought I was in dire straits. It mattered to me what they thought; I needed them so desperately.

The Welfare Department is at present having a hard time identifying our social class. They've been holding on to our medical-assistance application for more than six months; their usual time is six weeks. "Yours is a difficult case," we've been told—not as an excuse from the bureaucracy but as a reasonable explanation from our lawyer and our advocates at Inglis House. The Welfare Department doesn't know what to do with us. We're a middle-class family (two college professors, a couple of IRAs, children who might need to go to college)—how do we fit in? Even the system knows there's a question there.

Are well-spouses single, divorced, widowed? Are we dating? Are we grieving? Are we skilled or unskilled workers? The insurance companies say we're unskilled. Custodial. This way they don't have to cover home-health aides—neither me nor Benny nor Aurelio. In the hospital, however, "custodial" suddenly becomes highly skilled. Jeff was once moved onto a different floor because none of the nurses, not even the head nurse, wanted to take the responsibility of tending the respirator.

Friends also needed to know where we stood, perhaps because it had some bearing on where they stood. They would sometimes voice questions. "How do you do it?" "Do you sleep in the same room with him?" And Marielle, our grown social-worker daughter, said, "I can't understand it. You had that big family meeting and still nothing's happening?" She was almost in tears.

Still, the immediacy was mine alone. How seriously, for example, should I take my marriage vows? Did "in sickness and in health, till death do us part" mean me take care of Jeff? Did it mean toilet? Respirator? Twenty times a night? I'd thought it meant merely be with him. And how could I even be with him, when, in the midst of every serious conversation, there was always jar and toilet?

Why didn't anybody ever call me up and ask, in a concerned tone, "Did the attendant show up today?" Why didn't rich Uncle Carl, in answer to my letter, rush to the phone and assure me he and Aunt Phyllis would do all they could? They're so upper middle class, why weren't they shocked and appalled at the description of my life? How could he let his brother's daughter live this way? How could he allow his brother's grandchildren to live this way? How angry did I have a right to be? And why wasn't any of the family coming forth and nagging and insisting we at least consider a nursing home? If my mother were alive, what would she have said or done?

Where do we stand? Where do our children stand? During October 1991 I told everybody—good friends, mothers in the park, Jeff's parents, Jeff's doctor, our attendant—how great Bret, twelve, had been that first night with the respirator. How he wanted to be the one to do the first night, how interested and intelligent he was about all those arrows and dials, and that cute matter-of-fact look he'd get, those four or five times, when he'd have to adjust the "pillows" in his dad's nose or turn off the false alarm. And especially how, around 4:30 A.M., when the machine was delivering too many breaths per minute, he was the one who called the emergency number, and then he and Jeff collaborated on the problem and soon had it taken care of.

I told people proudly and excitedly, almost happily, and with love. But they, who usually adored Bret, who praised his precociousness, who gave him special kid treatment, merely shrugged or said "Uh-huh." And I thought, "Oh, my God, they expect him to do it. Just like they expect me to do it." I realized they couldn't give him (or me) the recognition that we were doing more than a terrific job because they were afraid he would catch on that he's doing a job he shouldn't be doing in the first place. And then maybe they'd have to do it, or part of it. "Oh, my God," I thought, more sadly than desperately. "They're doing it to my kids, too."

Today, I reconsider. Maybe it wasn't that. Probably they just didn't know what to make of it, a twelve-year-old kid doing respirator at 4:30 A.M. Probably they just didn't know where they, Bret, I, or it stood. And possibly that's also why some social workers say Uh-huh.

But still, why did Blue Cross pay $1,080 a month for the respirator but not even a fraction of that for a specialist to stay with Jeff and the respirator while it was in operation— namely nights? Why was the system so willing to shell out that kind of money for his sleep and none for mine? Was his sleep worth more? Did they know where he stood and not me? ■

Where did our home stand? If it was a home—not a zoo or an employment office or my work—why was I dealing with on-the-job stress minute by minute? Were our children being brought up in an institution? Was my husband already in a nursing home?

I received a few clues, a few answers. Once the social worker at the service told me that we were the only family her agency was funding; everyone else was either single or, as she put it, "married and the wife sends him back to Mama."

"I can understand why," I answered.

"So can I," she agreed.

But it felt like fishing for information. Or for compliments. Or for *more* compliments. The clues felt like other questions. Could I "send him back to Mama"? Would Mama take him? Could I leave him on Mama's doorstep? Could I leave him on anybody's doorstep? And mostly, was the service impressed wth me because I didn't send him back to Mama? Did that mean that, when funding got low, they'd put us last on the list for having our hours cut?

Okay, I'd think. It is *not* a solution to send him home to Mama, to Papa, or to either of his brothers or to any of his uncles. So why was it considered a solution for him to be in my home? Was I doomed to be awakened every hour for the rest of my life? Jeff would say he couldn't see any alternative. I'd say, "I can think of lots of alternatives." His mother some nights, his father, his brothers. Or no one; some nights he could just suffer. We could take turns suffering.

I was trying to gain perspective, to come from the beginning, to stop taking for granted what I'd been doing all these years and what I'd be doing for years after, maybe forever; I was trying to stop assuming that I was the solution. But, it was no use. I had been the solution too long. I was accustomed to being the solution. And perhaps that's what all the questions and ponderings were for, to move me toward getting unaccustomed. ∎

Photographer Anna Moon and I are collaborating on a photo/poetry exhibit and book. About a year ago Anna drove eight hours from upstate New York to meet me for the first time and to begin shooting photos of the care giver at home. When she showed me some of her other care-giver photos, I felt a little apprehensive and dubious; they reminded me of *Gramps,* that well-known photo collection of a young man who decided to be care giver to his dying grandfather. The photos spell out a kind of dignity that was not quite my message; they fail, at least for me, to show the side of the care-giver phenomenon that is bitter, sad, complaining, and considering change. When I saw Anna's photos of that other care giver, I wondered if she could relate to me, if I would be enough like the image in *Gramps.*

Gramps was a lot smaller and lighter than Jeff, and I wondered whether he woke up as many times at night, and whether he wanted everything to be done "slowly." Moreover, his grandson had chosen; he'd had a choice. As it turned out, Anna did not have a *Gramps* mind-set, but so caught up was I in my dire straits and in my need to know where I stood that I couldn't help feeling alienated and a bit uptight.

A very big piece of my dilemma was, Am I doing this by choice or by coercion? Sure, I had chosen this years back, but what about now? What about a month from now? What about a month ago? I felt I had constantly to reevaluate. If I had the choice now, would there soon come a point when I didn't? Or if I still had the choice but suddenly changed my mind, how would I go about implementing that change? If I mentioned these questions at well-spouse meetings, they'd say, "Can you afford a nursing home?" and "How are you going to pay for it?"

A year ago I did change my mind. There is always a lapse of time between when a well spouse decides it's nursing-home time and when it actually is nursing-home time, that is, when the ill spouse goes into a nursing home. That time period, to me, felt at least sometimes like slavery, or like rape.

The rape theme kept coming up. Jar began to feel like rape. Toilet had long ago begun to feel like rape. Was it rape? Was I allowing myself to be raped? Was I allowing myself to be a victim? How could I let that man treat me this way? He was just some kid I met on the bus; what gave him the right to make me wipe him?

A bad fantasy—a waking nightmare—occurred to me around the time Jeff was beginning to be unable to transfer to and from the trike. We're at an MS support-group meeting, and I'm the only one not in a wheelchair; in fact, I'm the only one who has the use of her hands. I'm in charge of jar and toilet for all of them; furthermore, I'm the only female in the group. They all turn out to be pigs. "Hey, Nursie," they go, "I need the jar. Oooo, oooo, hurry up! Oooo, oooo." "No, me first. I need it more." "No, no, me! Over here, Nursie." Then one of them commands the others' attention. "Er, excuse me, Ma'am. I have a motor disability, and I'm having trouble jerking off. Can you come over here and help me?" In the very worst version of that fantasy, I recognize the men as Jeff's old fraternity buddies and he turns to me and says, "Well? Can't you help out my friends?"

Politicians talk about "respite care." The MS Society talks about "respite care." Well-spouses talk about "respite care." Why did everyone seem to think respite care was enough? Every time I came back from a respite I'd walk in to toilet, and I'd need more respite. My shopping trip or poetry reading would recede very quickly. No amount of time off was enough. Jeff and I both wanted twenty-four-hour care, 365 days a year. Jeff did not want me to be his attendant; he wanted me to be his wife. He did not want me to look at him and think "Toilet." Toilet felt like rape to him, too. We were both being raped. How, I wrote in a letter to Hillary Rodham Clinton, can a disabled individual function as an individual, and how can a disabled family function as a family, unless the dependency relationship is, as completely as humanly possible, eliminated? Hillary's secretary answered with a form letter.

When I had the broken ankle, my in-laws came to help for a few days and then left. I wished that the service would temporarily increase our hours, or at least say they wished they could increase them. Why did Blue Cross provide a housekeeper for five hours a day and not twenty-four? (My ankle remained broken for twenty-four, and Jeff was at risk for toilet for twenty-four.) Why, for that matter, didn't they provide a housekeeper who could lift Jeff? In general, why did people, and professionals, keep leaving us? In particular, why did they keep leaving me alone with him? Did they have the right to do that? Did I have the right to refuse? Did I have the right to ask any of these questions? Where did I stand?

The questions needed answering. For one thing, even a chronic grief needs closure. But I also needed to know where I stood for practical reasons. I needed to make decisions. Should I go to work, for example—or rather, more work? "You can't work," said Freda. "You have enough on you. Really. Really, Mar." Most of my other friends advised similarly. But Jeff's mother said, "You do what you have to do." And my therapist said, "You'll like working. You'll see." For a long time I was afraid to take the chance. (And indeed, on my first day teaching at Temple, Benny mentioned that he was looking for another job, one with benefits.) You do what you have to do, but can you?

Ultimately—mainly—I needed to know where I stood so that I could make that all-important nursing-home decision.

The social worker from the service kept saying she was going to schedule a home visit to assess things. There seemed to be several delays, even when we reminded her. Was she stalling, afraid of what she'd find, that Jeff really was deadweight, as I'd reported? That she'd have to fund us for more expensive—and more impossible-to-find—care? That she'd have to advise nursing home? That Jeff wouldn't take to that advice?

Everybody was denying. Nobody knew what to do. It was a conspiracy of silence. Jeff's mother would call on the phone. "How are you?" "Fine," Jeff would say, and begin to report ordinary news.

I'd break in. "We are not fine. I just did toilet." I was determined to say that, or things like that. I wanted people to know what I did; I wanted to be acknowledged, if not praised. Besides, if people didn't know, I had no hope at all that they'd rescue us.

My therapist said, "I can see you've all had it." But that only meant new questions. Should we have had it? Is it soon enough for us to have had it? Have most people in our situation had it? Or is it our fault—my fault—that we've had it? What does that mean, to have had it? And should we—should I—work harder at not having had it?

Even when the therapist went on to say she thought Jeff

should be in a nursing home, my unarticulated question was, "And is that because we can't handle it?" ■

Part of going to well-spouse meetings and the annual convention was to search for the answer to that bottom-line question of where we stood. Many well spouses either had the same question or knew what I meant when I asked it. One of them stood up and said, "I'm not here for answers. I don't expect you to have answers. But I know you'll have the same questions."

I mentioned jail before, briefly. Jail seems to be a recurring metaphor among well spouses. Perhaps the very mention of it expresses how ludicrous and farfetched our situations are. I once read that prisoners who are dying have to keep serving their sentences, although activists are working to get the authorities to allow the ones who want to, and whose families want them, to die at home. I thoroughly approve of the activists' work, but when I read about it, another thought popped into my mind before I could control it. "So all I have to do is get Jeff to commit some crime and they wouldn't let him die at home; we wouldn't have to worry about Blue Cross or medical assistance; it would all be at the expense of the state."

But what crime? He can't use his hands, he can't even make a phone call unaided, he couldn't even arrange to hire someone to commit murder. What crime could he even be framed for? ■

I would, of course, think about the future. In words, my questions would include, How quickly will the MS progress? How much longer will he live? Will we eventually get more hours from the service? How bad does he—does it—have to get before he goes into a nursing home? Will our insurance cover at-home care?

But apart from the words, my feeling was that this was how it would always be. Nights, lifting, and toilet, with grandchildren instead of Devin playing with the bedpan. And if there were no grandchildren, I worried about whether we'd be able to attract attendants without kids around, whether cats would be enough, maybe we should get kittens. The dire straits would go on forever. Most of the time, that's what I assumed.

Of course, those dire straits did not go on forever. They got replaced by other dire straits.

The questions also escalated. How come, for example, that social worker never called me back? How come her supervisor never called me back? I mean again and again. And I told that secretary we were looking for free home-health aides—volunteers, grants, whatever; I said that repeatedly; I told her our family wasn't one of those who could afford thousands of dollars a week. I made it quite clear. So how come, weeks later, someone else from that organization got back to me with the names of three ordinary agencies I could have looked up in the phone book?

As time went on the MS got to Jeff's brain, or at least affected cognitive functions and memory. His solar dealings, mismanaging the service's forms, ordering expensive items from catalogs—was that cognitive stuff, or emotional? "Request a neuropsychological evaluation," a professional suggested. I did. "So I can know where I stand," I told his doctor. "And so I don't have to do a neuropsychological evaluation. Also, so I'll know whether or not to confiscate his catalogs." "Yes," that doctor agreed, "I'll mention it on his next visit." How come that never happened?

When Jeff was in rehab, why did every worker there seem to assume that he was an accident case? Why did they keep acting as if he had a choice about whether or not to move his right arm? Why were they always playing teacher—"easing the family into it," they probably call it. "Can you help me transfer him?" "Would you like to shave him?" I kept having to set them straight; "No, I would not like to shave him. I've been shaving him for seven years." Why wasn't that on his chart?

They were nice when Jeff and I informed them that we didn't want him to have an intermittent catheter, much less have them "teach the family" how to catheterize him. But if they hadn't been nice, could they have forced us to catheterize him? Could the law have forced us?

Hospitals seem to be more sophisticated than rehab centers. The hospital personnel understood when I told them we wouldn't be visiting very much, that this was our vacation from Jeff, a chance to recharge, go to the movies, play an uninterrupted game of Scrabble—and sleep. The one time a nurse asked me, "Can you wash his hair? We're terribly busy," and I answered, "I'm terribly busy, too, and I need a rest from washing his hair," she didn't seem offended. In the hospital they seemed to know I was in dire straits. But how come they kept sending him home?

What clinched it for me, what finally showed me where I stood, may have been the mix-ups. Especially the series of mix-ups that resulted when once Visiting Nurses said they'd called the insurance company and gotten thirty days of night nursing approved. Thirty consecutive nights of sleep! First, several nights their nurses didn't show, close to midnight when it was too late to find a replacement and when I could have had Jeff in bed an hour earlier. Then I had to be on the phone with the agency awhile. And of course, after that I could never relax on any night, even when they did show, because I never knew for sure. I certainly couldn't go to bed early. Not quite midway through the thirty days, the insurance company changed its mind or discovered some mistake; no more night nurses. I'd found out about such midstream changes when I broke my ankle, and many health-care workers had told me that kind of thing is fairly common. Yet Visiting Nurses acted surprised. "You deal in this kind of thing all the time; hasn't it happened before?" I asked. Very carefully, it seemed, the director answered, "Not in my experience." I still don't know if I should have believed her.

Several nights later at 11:30, a night nurse rang our bell. "They made a mistake," I had to tell her. "We've been cut off." I was tempted to let her in, but I knew that if I did, we'd be hit for something like three hundred dollars.

The message I got, repeatedly, was that nobody cared what I was going through—nobody, that is, who could do anything. It was okay with everybody if my back got ruined from lifting, if I died from sleep deprivation, and if our children were orphaned. They would let that happen. Nights, lifting, and toilet did not shock them; the more I did, the more they knew I could do. Nobody who was anybody seemed to realize how ludicrous the whole thing was.

(I recall Colette, another well spouse, shaking her head and murmuring, over and over, "Ludicrous. That's what my life is. Ludicrous.")

There were exceptions. I asked a repairwoman from the respirator company, on one of her several 3:30 A.M. visits to our house, "Must I be awakened like this? Is there any other way?"

This person did not say uh-huh. She did not keep mum. Instead she answered me honestly, acknowledging the ludicrousness. "Well, this woman I know, her husband's been sick for years, getting her up all hours of the night and all that. She was so stressed out she got on drugs and had to go into rehab; then they *had* to get somebody to take care of her husband. That's the only way I know . . . " She left the sentence dangling and threw up her arms; I loved her for that.

But by and large it felt as though they were all denying something, or maybe purposely keeping mum about some secret, some conspiracy. Someone, it seemed, gained by the silence and would lose by the breaking of that silence. Namely, if I stopped doing nights, lifting, and toilet, then that someone would have to start doing nights, lifting, and toilet, or find someone else to. So they kept to the silence, ready to stall me forever. ■

As often happened, a dream made the situation more clear and brought me closer to knowing where I stood. Our daughter Marielle was, in real life, getting married in a few months. She was, understandably, worried that something terrible would happen and her father wouldn't be able to get to the wedding, or that something would go wrong with him that would somehow prevent the wedding. I dreamt that it was the day and hour for which the ceremony was scheduled, and nobody but the maid of honor had shown up. Marielle was jilted by the groom and the guests. The thing was, no one would admit to this. They all just kept milling about. Time passed—five minutes, ten minutes, two hours. "Gee, people sure are late," said the maid of honor (like the attendant being six hours late). "Yes, they're pretty late today" (like Jeff being "in bad shape today"). Another hour passed. "Well, I guess we'll just have to have the wedding tomorrow," someone shrugged (like that social worker, "I'll get back to you tomorrow").

Through it all I was gasping. "But . . . but . . . what do you mean, late? A hundred and fifty people late, for a wedding? And the groom? You can't have it tomorrow"—I was practically in tears—"the date on the invitations is today."

I pondered what was happening as if it were a math problem. I went over several possibilities, including having made a mistake on the invitations. Finally I understood. This had to be a dream.

And so, I realized the next morning, did its real-life parallel, nights, lifting, and toilet. So did Jeff's living at home with us. It all had to be a dream. And I had to wake up from it.

"You have to wake up *to* it," Arin, twenty, said when I told him that dream.

It wasn't only that dream. The questions that amounted to Where do I stand? had begun to point to answers. I'd come to several conclusions that helped. "I'm willing for 'it' to be a *period* of my life," I wrote in my journal, "but I'm not willing for it to *be* my life. Seven years bad luck, okay. But not *eight* years."

A helpful formulation was "no-win situation." I was tired of the no-win situation, and the multitude of no-win situations that went along with it. "Get out from under" was another appropriate phrase. It was time to get out from under. Also helpful was something from a long-ago well-spouse newsletter by a woman who had decided to leave her ill spouse. "I love him very much," she wrote, "but my children have said to me, 'We don't need *two* ill parents.'"

Friends also helped me describe and define the situation. Anna described Jeff as "self-absorbed and childlike," and Roberta made the apt assessment "Jewish American prince." "Put your foot down," she said. Nancy, my friend who shared with me home schooling, writing, and an appreciation for not taking things for granted, told me gently, "There's always all this fuss about whether somebody should go into a nursing home, but then when he goes it works out just fine."

The social worker who worked with Jeff's doctor said to me, "Maybe the next time he goes into the hospital, he'll go from there right to Inglis House."

But he didn't say how, and I figured they'd take care of it. I didn't know there was something I was supposed to say and do.

Another misconception. I had been researching medical assistance, and the lawyer went over some of the details. We wouldn't lose the house; we wouldn't lose my IRAs; I'd have to look up Jeff's life-insurance policy to find out its

surrender value, his pension, our Blue Cross policy. I'd have
to get the medical-assistance application from Philadelphia
Corporation on Aging. One of the items on that application
involved looking up all our bank-account withdrawals for
the past two-and-a-half years; I'd have to account for anything over five hundred dollars. This all felt like cruel and
unusual punishment, and we were law-abiding citizens (despite all my speculations about jail). The main thing was
that no one thought to tell me that, while I was doing all
those things, Jeff could already be in a nursing home. I
wouldn't have had to do all that grueling and worrisome
stuff *and* nights, lifting, and toilet at the same time.

My wonderful social-worker daughter, Marielle, finally
gave me this information. "You have to tell them you're not
taking him home," she said. "It has to be in the hospital; it's
impossible to get anything done except *from the hospital.*
And you have to actually say, 'I'm not taking him home.'"
("I didn't know you could do that," other well spouses have
since said to me. Why weren't we told?)

I'd thought I had to help myself first, before God or anybody would help me. I hadn't known I could be helped first.
That was a very big answer to a very big question. And so
began the coda. It was not quite the end. I felt I had to call
every professional on Jeff's floor—the head doctor, head
nurse, his doctor again, his doctor's social worker again—to
tell them "I'm not taking him home." I added another magic
sentence that Elle had told me about. "I'd like to speak with
a social worker about it."

But why did they all listen to Jeff so much? Of course he
was resistant; of course he was scared; of course it would

take him time. Of course I, too, needed time. Yet they kept saying things like "He has to agree to it," "He doesn't seem to be in agreement," "The two of you don't agree," as though that were somehow my fault or a reflection on the state of the marriage.

I finally said another magic sentence, one I made up. "Yes, I know he doesn't yet agree, but I want you to push him to agree."

To Jeff I said more magic words. "It's not safe for you to live at home."

Given time and patience and assurance, Jeff valiantly bowed to circumstances. The kids and I are living, if not happily ever after, then non-ludicrously ever after. To put it more honestly, we are euphoric to be relieved of nights, lifting, and toilet.

Nancy said, "Yay!" Freda said, "Mazel tov." Roberta said, "Wonderful." And my well-spouse friend Fern said, very seriously, "I'm really happy for you, Marion."

My elation has not tapered off much. Evenings, the kids and I hang out with no interruptions—no "Toilet," no "Mar!" It feels like a party. Sometimes we make it into a party, with candy and ice cream. We play cards, Scrabble, go out to a movie. It feels great.

Jeff has also been doing well. Although there were adjustments, and he was scared. He had to wait three months for permanent placement in Inglis House at a regular "old-age home" where they seemed unfamiliar with MS, in particular unfamiliar with complete paralysis, and even more unfamiliar with patients who were research physicists. Still, those first few weeks, he and various colleagues wrote three physics papers, and he received a phone call from Mentor Technologies. Would he do some consulting work on global positioning systems? They came to his room at the nursing home and, like his other colleagues, took dictation. Recently someone at Inglis House has been interested in his solar-collector invention and is working with him to form a business.

He has good nurse's aides and bad ones. At the support group he belongs to, the residents were estimating the proportion; Jeff estimated 66⅔ percent to 33⅓ percent, with the "bad ones" concentrated in the morning shift. Most of the workers I meet are fine; Dolores and I chat a lot; Vince and Jeff are good friends, and once when Vince was out with the flu he called Jeff to say hi. The last time I visited, though, the aide on duty seemed so insultingly grim I felt sad. In general, Jeff can't be expected to be thrilled or even happy, but his health is definitely better than it would have been had he remained at home. Except for two incidents with the feeding tube coming loose, he has not been hospitalized at all.

Sometimes it's a drag to visit him twice a week. Because he feels he's not getting enough physical therapy, every Sunday and Thursday, I do half an hour of arm and leg lifting, counting to twenty, and "slowly." Jeff understands, though, how I feel about visiting. "I remember," he says, "how I used to feel visiting you when you had the babies."

Actually, our visits are good. We don't find it difficult to pass the time; we have plenty of things to talk about, and it still seems to be true that, when I'm feeling good about something, he's the one I'm excited to tell, and when I'm feeling bad about something, he's the one who can best support and comfort me. It's definitely true, as I'd expected it would be, that I am able to feel more and more compassion for him as the months pass. I am also able and willing to be loving. I'm no longer running for my own life.

Devin, who comes along with me on at least half of the visits, doesn't find them difficult either. He's made friends with Vince, who loves his drawings, and with Bob, another resident, who gives him (and me) sandwiches, bananas, and soda. He goes to Friends on Wheels, the support-group meetings, with Jeff and me. Arin goes in every Tuesday and writes down physics calculations. Bret and Marielle visit every two or three weeks; when they do we make it a family affair and go out, afterwards, to an Indian restaurant we all love that's on the way home. Jeff cannot go along.

When Jeff first stopped living at home, I decided to give myself at least a year to relax and recover, and to enjoy the freedom and the sleep. I decided not to push myself to make any decisions or take any actions concerning, for example, job hunting or new writing projects. That year is almost up, and as usual I am ahead of schedule. (No more "slowly" for me!) I've decided to increase my course load at Temple, teaching two calculus classes back to back, and I am applying for full-time employment, though I'm in no hurry. To this end, and also because I now have time for math (my first great love), I've been studying set theory and working on a problem concerning partially ordered sets. I'm also working on a theory begun back when I was in high school that involves a generalization of ordinary arithmetic. I love it all. In general, I'm working on thinking more professionally and less as a downtrodden human being. I'm beginning to think of myself as a provider for my children, a feeling I enjoy.

I also am experiencing some of the joys of the single life. I don't mean other men. I mean, for example, table lamps. Jeff never liked them. He worried about the kids knocking them over or getting burned. All our lamps were attached to the walls, usually with plastic plugs. One day a few months ago, at a yard sale in the neighborhood, for five dollars I bought a sleek golden lamp with four babies dancing around the base. Two other table lamps followed that same week from American Thrift. They lit up corners, adding warmth as well as light.

I continue to go to well-spouse support-group meetings; three others in the group have spouses in nursing homes. I'm no longer in dire straits, but I am still a well spouse.

Aurelio still lives with us. As a single mother would, I need him. He alternates with Arin watching Devin while I go to teach or out to lunch with friends, and he helps me keep up with the laundry (or, we would joke, I help him keep up with the laundry). He fixes machines when they break, he does the living-room floor (the part of housework I hate most), and he goes thrifting with us and plays Scrabble. The family bed now takes a new form; every evening Aurelio and I mock fight over who "gets" Devin. "I'll tell you a story," coaxes Aurelio. "I'll sing you lullabies," I counter.

Some of my friends say I look "so much better—less tired, more relaxed."

I frown. "But that's what you used to say before. I'd say

'Jeff got me up every five minutes last night,' and you'd say 'Well, you don't look it.' "

"I thought you didn't *then*," they answer, "but now I see the difference."

A surprising and pleasant development has been that at Inglis House the nurses and social workers don't say uh-huh. Instead they ask, "How did you do it? However did you do it?" "You're the talk of the floor," the head nurse once told me. "Everyone here admires you so much for doing this for so many years."

Several weeks ago, giving a presentation about the Well Spouse Foundation to a large group of professionals, I mentioned "twenty times a night" and they did not look askance or murmur uh-huh. Instead, a single loud gasp traveled around the room.

Maybe the difference is that when you say "I *am* waking up twenty times a night," they're not willing to hear it, but when you say "I *was* waking up twenty times a night," they are. Or maybe, now that I'm no longer an at-home care giver, I'm viewed in a more professional light. Rightly or wrongly, I'm now sort of in their league. Or maybe I present things differently. Why the sudden change, why the sudden lifting of the conspiracy of silence, I don't know. I do know, however, that I like the lifting.

I wish the professionals—in particular, the social workers—had been more aggressive all along. I wish that right from the beginning, sixteen-and-a-half years ago when Jeff was first diagnosed, we had been taken aside and, gently and realistically and with dignity, informed as to the range of scenarios we could expect over the years and decades—including nights, lifting, and toilet. I wish, over those years and decades, we had been taken aside again and again and kept informed about the various options and their limitations, offered advance information about at-home and nursing-home care and the particulars involved. And I wish they had informed themselves about us; I wish, especially, they had known and acknowledged when we reached the point of dire straits.

And I wish that I had been taken aside alone. "How are you doing?" I should have been asked, and perhaps, "Do you really want to keep doing this?" In other words, I wish they had told, or asked, me where I stood. ∎

Two months after Jeff's last day living at home Marielle got married. It was, as she and her husband, Matt, described it many times afterwards, their "dream wedding." Unlike the wedding in my surrealistic dream of months back, the vast majority of the guests showed up. The bridesmaids showed up. And the groom showed up. People were not even late.

Her father also showed up. We had hired Benny to go to the nursing home and deliver him. True, Benny wound up drinking more than a little too much and getting more than tipsy; Aurelio had to accompany them on the trip back to the nursing home. Jeff, handsome and alert upon arrival, got overheated somewhere along the way, and I was the only one who noticed and who thought to remove his jacket; in that commotion I missed my sister's toast, which mentioned my late mother.

But Marielle didn't miss that toast, or anything else.

Jeff's MS neither prevented nor spoiled her wedding. When, around 2:30 A.M., I arrived home from the after-wedding party given by Matt's parents, I was conscious not of any lonely feeling, but of the joys of coming back to a house in which I would be able to fall into, and stay in, a blissful sleep. ■

A nonsurreal life feels wonderful. Knowing where I stand feels wonderful. Having so many of my questions answered feels wonderful. I was in dire straits. The straits were dire enough. It was just-terrible. It was untenable. I had a right to call for help. I had a right to be rescued. I had the right to rescue myself. I am not the only solution. I had the right to burn out.

And yes, Arin, it's over. The government didn't quite decide that we'd had enough, but it did agree that we'd had enough. It's over. No more nights, lifting, and toilet. I woke up from it. I woke up *to* it. I can wake up now. I'm allowed to sleep, and I'm allowed to wake up. ■

resources

■ THE FAMILY CAREGIVER ALLIANCE, 425 Bush Street, Suite 500, San Francisco, CA 94108; 415/434-3388 (in California, 800/445-8106); free information on caring for people with adult-onset brain disorders (for example, stroke, Parkinson's, Alzheimers).

■ NATIONAL ASSOCIATION OF AREA AGENCIES ON AGING, 1112 16th Street, NW, Suite 100, Washington, D.C. 20036; 800/677-1116; referrals to state or local agencies for help in finding services for you or your spouse and other family members, including respite care and help with nutrition and transportation.

■ NATIONAL FAMILY CAREGIVERS ASSOCIATION, 9621 East Bexhill Drive, Kensington, MD 20895; 301/942-6430; support, advocacy, quarterly newsletter, access to network of other care givers, $15 annual membership fee.

■ WELL SPOUSE FOUNDATION, Box 801, New York, NY 10023; 800/838-0879 (in New York, 212/644-1241); $20 fee includes membership, bimonthly newsletter, information on conferences and support groups throughout the United States.

167

ADG.3425

RC
377
C54
1996

8/29/96